Scarecrow Studies in Young Adult Literature
Series Editor: Patty Campbell

Scarecrow Studies in Young Adult Literature is intended to continue the body of critical writing established in Twayne's Young Adult Authors Series and to expand it beyond single-author studies to explorations of genres, multicultural writing, and controversial issues in YA reading. Many of the contributing authors of the series are among the leading scholars and critics of adolescent literature, and some are YA novelists themselves.

The series is shaped by its editor, Patty Campbell, who is a renowned authority in the field, with a thirty-year background as critic, lecturer, librarian, and teacher of young adult literature. Patty Campbell was the 2001 winner of the ALAN Award, given by the Assembly on Adolescent Literature of the National Council of Teachers of English for distinguished contribution to young adult literature. In 1989 she was the winner of the American Library Association's Grolier Award for distinguished service to young adults and reading.

1. *What's So Scary about R.L. Stine?* by Patrick Jones, 1998.
2. *Ann Rinaldi: Historian and Storyteller,* by Jeanne M. McGlinn, 2000.
3. *Norma Fox Mazer: A Writer's World,* by Arthea J.S. Reed, 2000.
4. *Exploding the Myths: The Truth about Teens and Reading,* by Marc Aronson, 2001.
5. *The Agony and the Eggplant: Daniel Pinkwater's Heroic Struggles in the Name of YA Literature,* by Walter Hogan, 2001.
6. *Caroline Cooney: Faith and Fiction,* by Pamela Sissi Carroll, 2001.
7. *Declarations of Independence: Empowered Girls in Young Adult Literature, 1990–2001,* by Joanne Brown and Nancy St. Clair, 2002.
8. *Lost Masterworks of Young Adult Literature,* edited by Connie S. Zitlow, 2002.

Lost Masterworks of Young Adult Literature

Edited by
Connie S. Zitlow

*Scarecrow Studies in
Young Adult Literature, No. 8*

The Scarecrow Press, Inc.
Lanham, Maryland, and Oxford
2002

SCARECROW PRESS, INC.

Published in the United States of America
by Scarecrow Press, Inc.
A Member of the Rowman & Littlefield Publishing Group
4720 Boston Way, Lanham, Maryland 20706
www.scarecrowpress.com

12 Hid's Copse Road
Cumnor Hill, Oxford OX2 9JJ, England

Copyright © 2002 by Connie S. Zitlow

All rights reserved. No part of this publication may be reproduced, stored in a retrieval system, or transmitted in any form or by any means, electronic, mechanical, photocopying, recording, or otherwise, without the prior permission of the publisher.

British Library Cataloguing in Publication Information Available

Library of Congress Cataloging-in-Publication Data

Lost masterworks of young adult literature / edited by Connie S. Zitlow.
     p. cm. — (Scarecrow studies in young adult literature ; 8)
Includes bibliographical references and index.
  ISBN 0-8108-4360-9 (hardcover : alk. paper)
  1. Young adult literature, American—History and criticism. 2. Young adult literature, English—History and criticism. I. Zitlow, Connie S., 1942- II. Series.
  PS490 .L68 2002
  810.9'9283—dc21
                                                                                               2002004839

Printed in the United States of America

∞™ The paper used in this publication meets the minimum requirements of American National Standard for Information Sciences—Permanence of Paper for Printed Library Materials, ANSI/NISO Z39.48-1992

Contents

Foreword   ix
   Marc Talbert

Acknowledgments   xiii

Introduction   xv
   Connie S. Zitlow

1 *Noah's Castle* by John Rowe Townsend: A World Too Nasty to Miss out on   1
   Virginia Euwer Wolff

2 Bobby Marks Redux: Reconsidering Robert Lipsyte's *Summer Rules* and *The Summerboy*   6
   Michael Cart

3 Welcome Back, Smith! Four Leon Garfield Masterpieces   11
   Katherine Paterson

4 A Southern Voice Recalled: Two Novels by Mildred Lee   17
   Sue Ellen Bridgers

5 A Gringo Comes of Age in the Southwest: Richard Bradford's *Red Sky at Morning*   22
   Chris Crowe

6 Real Stories, Real Voices: The Lost Works of Janet Bode   27
   Teri S. Lesesne

7	Gleeps, or a Case for Trixie Belden *Kathleen Krull*	31
8	*The Last Mission* by Harry Mazer: Heroism and Hell in World War II *John Noell Moore*	37
9	*Sex Education* by Jenny Davis: Lessons in Caring and Healing *Ann Wilder*	42
10	Opening Up: *The Secret Diary of Adrian Mole Aged 13¾* by Sue Townsend *Alleen Pace Nilsen*	46
11	Belonging to a Place: *Home Before Dark* by Sue Ellen Bridgers *Connie S. Zitlow*	51
12	The Law and Magic: Searching for Incantations in Sol Stein's *The Magician* *Margaret J. Ford and Susan L. Stevens*	57
13	Sharon Bell Mathis's *Listen for the Fig Tree*: A Timeless YA Novel *Pamela Sissi Carroll*	63
14	Humanity and Its Discontents in *The Keeper of the Isis Light* by Monica Hughes *Leila Christenbury*	68
15	Two Forgotten Novels by Bruce Clements *Kenneth L. Donelson*	73
16	Aidan Chambers's *Breaktime*: A Lost Masterwork by a Found Master Craftsman *Ted Hipple*	79
17	About Living On: *Sheila's Dying* by Alden Carter *Pam Muñoz Ryan*	85
18	*Send No Blessings* and *The Year of the Gopher*: Phyllis Reynolds Naylor's Lost Masterpieces about Setting One's Own Course *Lois T. Stover*	88

19	Finding One's Place in the World: *The Catalogue of the Universe* by Margaret Mahy *Patricia P. Kelly*	93
20	Portrait of Abuse: *Cages of Glass, Flowers of Time* by Charlotte Culin *Cindy Dobrez*	98
21	*The Quartzsite Trip* by William Hogan: A Life-Changing Week *Joni Richards Bodart*	103
22	Her Own Way: Pragmatic Abstinence in Norma Fox Mazer's *Up in Seth's Room* *Jennifer Hubert*	108
23	"We Cut Ourselves": Revisiting *Crosses* by Shelley Stoehr *Patrick Jones*	112
24	*Blinded by the Light* by Robin Brancato: A Forgotten Masterwork *Robert C. Small*	116
25	Searching for Identity and Reconciliation: *In Summer Light* by Zibby Oneal *Patricia L. Daniel and Joan F. Kaywell*	121
26	Some Thoughts on My First Novel Going out of Print *Marie G. Lee*	126
Index		130
About the Editor		133

Foreword

I congratulate you on reading this book, albeit before the fact. Likely, you have decided to read it because you have an interest in books for children and, specifically, an interest in young adult books that have gone out of print, that have been pronounced commercially dead by their publishers. Further, I assume that you have decided to read this book because you believe there exist a great many young adult books that should not have gone out of print, that should not have died—perhaps, even, books you grew up with and that had a great influence on your outlook for life, both young adult and adult.

If I have described your reasons for reading this book, you will be in the company of many kindred spirits for the next couple of hours.

It is always painful to see a much-loved book go out of circulation. To surrender to the power of a book is to invite a story and its characters into your very soul. Great books can bring color to emotions gone drab, energy to beliefs that are flagging, music to laughter gone hollow, companionship to hopes and dreams that are overwhelmed by isolation. Great books can provide shelter for those who are desperate for safe haven from the colliding storms of the past, the present, and the future. Especially the violent storm of the present.

To learn that a great book is lost is to feel less powerful in our daily battles against the onslaught of a predatory culture and the corrosiveness of time. To learn that a great book has gone out of print is to be reminded of our mortality, because something we have made an intimate part of our emotional selves has been declared, by the publishing world and the culture at large, to be obsolete.

It is especially hard for authors to see one of their own books go out of print. Many authors secretly consider having a book published to be one way of eluding the mortality that stalks us all. For many authors, writing books—those lumpy, sharp-cornered progeny of the mind—is the artistic and intellectual equivalent of having children who will carry into the future a treasured part of their unique genetic makeup. In their heads, authors, like all of us, know it is impossible to elude, or escape, death. But in the marrow of their bones, many authors, like so many of us, simply cannot comprehend their own deaths. And so, authors create books—just as architects create buildings, entrepreneurs create fortunes, musicians create symphonies—often in defiance of death itself.

So much blood and sweat and tears go into the writing of a book that, for many authors, having one of their books go out of print is the literary equivalent of a parent burying a child. But let's not go overboard. A book is not a son or a daughter, nor is a writer its parent. It is good to keep these things in proper perspective, especially because most writers live to see most, if not all, of their books go out of print. It is simply a fact of publishing life. That it happens sooner today in the life of most books, and less graciously, does not alter the fact that 99.9 percent of all books will go out of print eventually—usually within ten or twenty years, which is a generous statistic.

What books from the nineteenth century continue to be actively published? Precious few. What will be the attrition in 2102 for books currently published in the year 2002? Almost total. The books that survive will undoubtedly be great books. But does it follow that books that don't survive the vagaries of publishing within the next one hundred years are less great? In most cases, yes. But not always. Many out-of-print books are every bit as good as the books that stay in print.

And so, we must be concerned with what happens to good books, masterpieces even, that go out of print. The title of the book you now hold implies that out-of-print books are lost. This suggests that they are hidden/buried/lost in some dusty, web-shrouded literary cemetery—a library, perhaps—in which their spines act as gravestones, recording author and title and publisher—waiting for whatever literary archaeologist is lucky enough to happen upon them. Is this so bad? There are many more great books residing in libraries than are available to buy in bookstores.

You will think it odd, but I often think of libraries when I am visiting a cemetery, and cemeteries when I am visiting a library. I happen to love cemeteries as much as I love libraries. When I go to a cemetery, I am struck, almost always, by the solemnity, the quiet, the dignity of the place. Life's most profound questions well up in my mind, and I feel as if I am in the presence of people who, if they could talk, would give me useful answers to those questions.

As I walk along rows of gravestones, I read names, sometimes saying them aloud, noting dates, calculating ages, smiling at inscriptions and designs carved into stone or painted on wood. After a few moments, my mind begins to race with images and questions. Who were these people? What did they look like? Who loved them and who did they love? How did they walk, talk, laugh, cry? What did they like to eat best? Did they face death bravely? Were they scared or caught off guard? In answer to these questions, stories begin to fill my head. Faces appear. And voices. I feel the same joy that comes when I am in the thick of writing a novel.

Cemeteries ignite my imagination—the part of me that is a writer, surely, but more importantly the part of me that is most connected to the humanity I share with the living and the dead. So do books in a library. My imagination craves books good enough to spark it. And books require my imagination, and yours, in order to be resurrected from their inert state on shelves, in order to come to life.

But here the comparison between lost books and dead people begins to crumble. The body of an out-of-print book does not decompose like that of a dead human. Further, a book can continue to tell its own story long after it is out of print. The style of writing found on its pages may be different than what we are used to and its setting may be unfamiliar. But the questions it asks, the issues it tackles, the basic humanity of its characters will all be the same as in the books we can buy today. How better to understand our own times than to see life's great questions and issues and our shared humanity from another frame of reference, another time and place, and in language foreign enough to force us to listen more closely?

Books don't die, and cannot be lost, so long as there are people who understand the value of good books, in print or out of print, current or declared obsolete by publishers. And in this age of electronic books and on-demand printing technology, there is even less reason to believe books must die when they go out of print. In fact, there may be a time when books will never go out of print, at least technically or technologically, when they will be conjured, ghost-like, onto a computer screen or, in the flesh, as freshly printed words on paper.

In the following pages you will read essays by people who understand the value of good books, in particular young adult books, and who write convincingly about the immortality of particular books. As you read these essays, it will be good for you to remember that immortality for a book is not inherent. Immortality is bestowed on books by readers, such as yourself. After you finish this book, do your part to bequeath a tiny glimmer of immortality on young adult books dear to you, books that were given up for lost, when in fact they were not lost—a whole lot of readers were lost, instead.

In helping bequeath immortality to a book that has become an essential part of who you are, I believe that you elude, if only for a moment, the mortality that stalks us all. My head may tell me this isn't possible. But, in the marrow of my writer's bones, I believe it is so.

Marc Talbert

Marc Talbert has written many award-winning novels for children and young adults, a handful of which have been published in up to seven countries. Among them are *Dead Birds Singing, Heart of a Jaguar, A Sunburned Prayer,* and *Toby.* Most of his novels have gone out of print, but those that have are all now available on demand as Authors Guild Backinprint.com Editions. Talbert lives in Tesuque, New Mexico, with his wife and two daughters, and their many animals. For more details on his life and work, visit marctalbert.com.

Acknowledgments

I am extremely grateful to Patty Campbell for her idea, her support, and for her enthusiasm that seemed to increase with each stage of this project. I feel great appreciation to the incredible group of people who have enthusiastically written the essays that comprise this book. And always, I thank my family for their loving support.

Introduction

"Is there a work of literature for young adults that is a favorite of yours, a book that is out of print, or not readily available, or frequently overlooked? Is it lost to the attention of many young readers and the adults who read and promote this literature as a worthy and enjoyable genre of literary works?" I asked these questions of award-winning authors, teachers, librarians, professors of education and English, consultants, and literary critics—all who are in one way or another scholars and proponents of the genre we call young adult literature. Their resounding responses fill the pages of this book.

The contributors who have written about their favorite lost books in these twenty-six chapters include some renowned authors of works I return to again and again, scholars whose books and articles I read and use in my teaching, friends from the Assembly on Literature for Adolescents of the National Council of Teachers of English, and members of the Young Adult Library Services Association. Regardless of how we might classify our work and professional affiliation, what is most important is that we are first of all readers who have discovered the joys of quality literature, and we have favorite books that have left a particular impact on us and on other readers. We know how much the stories of young adults matter, how our lives are enriched by books, and we honor those, who, with their literary artistry, bring alive the experiences of others and help us see our own lives more clearly. We know what it means to be immersed in a book and want to share it with others. We know, in the words of Gary Salvner, "that literature has the capacity to enter our lives, to interact with what we already know and believe, and perhaps even to change us" (9). But the books must be available, and they must have readers.

The books chosen as *Lost Masterworks of Young Adult Literature* received critical acclaim when first published and are literary works that still tell compelling stories. Yet in one way or another, these books are lost. In each chapter, contributors have written about the value of an individual book or series of books. We have noted what the literary strengths are that make the work a young adult book of merit and why we think the story has the potential to appeal to teen readers today. Most of all, we have explored what about the lost work has the capacity to work its way into readers' thinking—what makes it a story one can care about.

How did *Lost Masterworks* come to be? It happened rather quickly, beginning with Patty Campbell's idea and her question, "Connie, would you be interested in putting together a book on lost YA works?" We (and many of the people whose chapters make up this book) were in Milwaukee where I was chairing the 2000 ALAN Workshop. Along with many other lovers of YA literature, we had just spent two days listening to leading authors talk about their own work and how literature matters to them and to young readers. We had discussed books with friends and new acquaintances, recommended favorites, and learned more about how we might use certain books in our classrooms and libraries. I was feeling a combination of emotions—joy and exhilaration, as the event I had planned was coming to a close, and the grief that surrounded us as we paid tribute to Robert Cormier during the time he would have spoken at the workshop. Before we left Milwaukee, I discovered there are many people who have a favorite "lost" book that they would like to be once again a "found" work.

The chapters they have written tell about books with a variety of topics, themes, settings, and modes. We begin with the opening chapter in which Virginia Euwer Wolff writes about John Rowe Townsend's dystopian novel set in an uncertain future in England and end with Marie G. Lee's thoughts about her first novel going out of print. Here are the voices of YA authors who would like specific works written by others to be no longer lost. Michael Cart conveys the thematic relevance of Robert Lipsyte's Bobby Marks stories with their "evergreen humor," and Katherine Paterson welcomes back characters in four reissued novels written by Leon Garfield. Sue Ellen Bridgers recalls the southern voice in two novels by Mildred Lee. Kathleen Krull makes a case for the Trixie Belden series, and Pam Muñoz Ryan wonders why Alden Carter's *Sheila's Dying* is out of print.

Lost Masterworks include many different genres. Teri Lesesne reminds us that many nonfiction works are lost, such as the real stories of Janet Bode. A science fiction work, *The Keeper of the Isis Light* by Monica Hughes, is one of Leila Christenbury's favorites of any genre. Alleen Pace Nilsen does a booktalk on a story told in diary format, Sue Townsend's *The Secret Diary of Adrian Mole Aged 13¾*. Amused by two forgotten books by Bruce Clements, Kenneth L. Donelson wonders why teachers pay so little attention to humorous novels. In contrast, Margaret J. Ford and Susan L. Stevens write about how Sol Stein's stark work of realism, *The Magician*, connects to the events of today. Some contributors write about books that are not out of print, but are too often overlooked, such as Richard Bradford's *Red Sky at Morning*, a favorite of Chris Crowe's. John Noell Moore would like to see Harry Mazer's work of historical fiction, *The Last Mission*, used in classrooms with other novels about war.

Included in various chapters are numerous examples of the literary versatility and artistry of authors of young adult literature. Using dialogue from *Breaktime*, Ted Hipple shows Aidan Chambers' extraordinary ability with language. Stories that transcend their specific settings are clearly noteworthy as Patricia P. Kelly points out in her discussion of the magic realism in Margaret Mahy's *The Catalogue of the Universe*, set in New Zealand. For me, Sue Ellen Bridgers' beautiful *Home Before Dark* reaches far beyond its setting in the tobacco fields of eastern North Carolina. Ann Wilder knows the impact Jenny Davis' *Sex Education* can have on students, and Pamela Sissi Carroll recalls how readers responded to Sharon Bell Mathis' *Listen for the Fig Tree*.

Several chapters focus on examples of lost masterworks with themes about identity, finding one's place in the world, and making decisions—a key part of much young adult literature. Lois T. Stover writes about two of Phyllis Reynolds Naylor's books. Patricia L. Daniel and Joan F. Kaywell have chosen a work by Zibby Oneal, and Jennifer Hubert reminds us about a story written by Norma Fox Mazer. Cindy Dobrez, Joni Richards Bodart, and Robert C. Small tell about lost books with the hard topics of abuse, death, and the allure of cults. Patrick Jones revisits Shelley Stoehr's *Crosses* as a book that paved the way for later works.

Here are stories of romance, humor, adventure, and tragedy, stories with exciting plot structures, powerful figurative language, and rich characterization portrayed from various points of view. As Michael Cart has asked, "Do they offer wisdom—or knowledge, at least, which is the beginning of wisdom; are they artfully written; are they successful in aesthetic terms; and are they entertaining; do they amuse; heck, are they just fun to read?" (Cart, 251). We invite you as readers to rediscover these books and perhaps think about some of your own favorite but "lost" stories that deserve to become once again "found."

BIBLIOGRAPHY

Cart, Michael. *From Romance to Realism: 50 Years of Growth and Change in Young Adult Literature*. New York: HarperCollins, 1996.

Salvner, Gary. (2001). "Lessons and Lives: Why Young Adult Literature Matters." *The ALAN Review* 28, no. 3: 9-13.

Chapter One

Noah's Castle by John Rowe Townsend: A World Too Nasty to Miss out on

Virginia Euwer Wolff

Whenever I read a dystopian novel, my insides get squirrely. Embattled between "This could never happen here" and "This might happen right here tomorrow!"—my reading becomes a weirdly oscillating experience. And it gets my heart rate right up.

John Rowe Townsend has set *Noah's Castle* (first published in 1975) in England in an uncertain future. Inflation is nearing the berserk range, food shortages affect everyone, winter is coming on, and Norman Mortimer, husband and father, has an idea that seems to him to be perfectly sound and unimpeachably honorable: He buys a big, old, unfriendly house and secretly converts its basement into a huge storage room; he stockpiles massive amounts of food and household supplies, and then moves his family into their new home, without telling them about the hoard in the cellar. England may starve, but the Mortimers will survive.

Dad Mortimer is steely, secretive, fiercely driven. And so sure he's right. Mother is meek because that's the way Dad likes her to be.

Like young people everywhere, the Mortimer sons and daughters have to discover what is going on and figure out what to do about it, almost simultaneously.

Food riots, vandalism, chaos ripping the community apart—all these seem inevitable as the story unfolds. Except that for young readers they're not. For those in the United States, *Noah's Castle* is likely to be the first experience of famine and the collapse of the social order.

Although Mr. Mortimer's hoarding stands at the storm center of the story, it's the young Mortimers who absorb our attention. Barry, our sixteen-year-old narrator, finds out that Father is trading shoes from his store to the butcher for a freezer full of meat (with lamb chops at £200), while both shoe store and butchery are claiming to be out of goods. The children hear on the radio that hoarding is now illegal. Thus, Dad's a criminal. Little Ellen, age eight, innocently takes two cans of ham from the basement cache to a child's birthday party. The neighborhood children and their families wonder where the ham came from, and if there is any more. Seventeen-year-old Nessie complains: "Why can't we just be in the same boat as everybody else? Oh, I hate concealment. I hate it, hate it, hate it!" (62). Barry, who has been sent to do Father's shopping at the butchery, wrestles with his guilt. And this from Geoff, age fifteen: "While you two are tripping over your consciences, I get on with it" (64).

A serious mess.

A loaf of bread soon costs £2500, the poor and the sick can't stand in the enormous queues in the chilling winter weather, armored cars must escort food delivery trucks, newspapers suspend publication, trains fail to run, and looting begins. The story reaches nearly Shakespearean proportions as most civic systems disintegrate, paralyzing the body politic, and starvation comes to the Mortimers' doorstep.

Will Barry Mortimer and his siblings do the right thing? What is the right thing? And is doing just a little bit of the right thing enough? At the heart of the story, the moral questions gnaw.

It's the task of the dystopian novel, the grown-up cautionary tale, to scare us into awareness. But dystopian novels haven't always given us fully fascinating, multi-dimensional characters that are just as complicated and elusive as the people we meet in real life. Many of these novels have earned their reputations on a lot of shock and only the most sketchily-drawn human behavior: Good people, bad people, weak people and strong, tenuously carried along by a story that drives its message home in a vehicle made of hard ironies.

Not so with *Noah's Castle*.

Mr. Mortimer appears at first to be simply rigid, domineering, low on impulse-control, high in engineering skills (the family basement is amazing), obsessive. His style as a father is largely inherited from his earlier years in the military. Barry asks him about the illegal gun he is polishing in secret at 5:30 a.m., and Dad replies, "it's not your business to interrogate me" (75). If this proud pariah's suffocating vision were not at the core of his family's gripping story, he would be funny.

As Mr. Mortimer questions none of his decisions, his loved ones begin to question all of them. His power to divide the family hinges on the resonant character depth in each family member. One of the very satisfying things about this book is its gender distribution. One father, one mother, two sons, two daughters, and we get to experience significant, eye-opening evolution in every one of them. Father repeatedly trivializes and scorns women and women's minds, but it's Nessie, his older daughter, whose brave rebellion catalyzes much of the movement of the story. Add to this mix a blackmailing neighbor and a parasitic houseguest who moves in with the family, who allows himself to be fed and pampered for months, and then threatens with icy subtlety to betray their shameful secret. It's this presumptuous miscreant who finally ignites Mother's will, and she takes action in a most believable way. We've been waiting for her to do so. Thanks to John Rowe Townsend's thoroughly convincing insights, there isn't a false note as these family members, acting on a full range of emotions, keep the pages turning.

In every story, the reader must be provoked to wonder, "What would I do if this were my life?" When the disorder that Mr. Mortimer has tried with all his heart to fortify his family against actually occurs, little by little and then in a terrifying siege, we can't help wondering what we would do in their places.

The teaching possibilities with *Noah's Castle* are vast: Anxiety graphs, intimidation charts, definitions of "loyalty," family meal planning, imaginary jury trial, dramatic role-playing; newspaper, film and video pieces; interrupt-the-story-and-tell-it-your-way exercises. Lessons in economics: What is inflation, actually? What is the math of the way it affects our own families? Lessons in populist movements: Why do they inevitably split into factions? Lessons in family dynamics: How does love manifest itself here? Students can eagerly immerse themselves in these activities.

They'll come naturally to the moral questions. Young people just do.

The title is, of course, an open invitation to think allegory, and for young readers embarking on their first allegorical literary venture, the fact that Mr. Mortimer's castle is actually high on a hill called the Mount is a potent opportunity to say, "Oh, I get it! Like Noah!" Needing so poignantly to upstage the Old Testament, Mr. Mortimer says to Barry, "I've got things old Noah wouldn't have dreamed of. You can bet your boots he didn't have dried milk or concentrated orange juice or macaroni . . ." (36). Or a deep freeze or a generator.

Barry is an alert, trustworthy narrator whose readers can go along with him every centimeter of the way as he learns what desperate measures people will take in desperate times. The arresting comparison between the son who journeys toward self-knowledge and the father who refuses such a journey is all the more compelling because both of them activate our empathy.

In the end Mr. Mortimer, weakened and chastened, transforms a cultural cliché (the super-controlling father) into a living, breathing, struggling man whose stiff upper lip trembles just as much as any of ours would.

If Norman Mortimer got his style from the world of the military, where did he get his values? There's the rub. He clearly got them from a society that has traditionally rewarded its men in direct proportion to how well they take care of their families. Wasn't Mr. Mortimer doing the right thing after all?

In the end he asks that question.

The child in me who is reading a story believes an author hasn't finished writing it till I've read the last page. By the time I reached *Noah's Castle's* last page, I'd known for a long time that Mr. Mortimer is easier to villify than to understand. But I hadn't anticipated that this last page, with its inescapable pathos, would cause me to weep for him.

The closeness of the three teens' births seems to have crucial plot reverberations. Could it be that Mr. Mortimer, in his final whimper, is telling us all that he actually understands the selfishness that prompted him to impregnate his submissive wife three years in a row, and his household hoarding was his attempt to take care of the large family he has sired?

What happens when the floor slides out from under us has become the basic fabric of young adult literature. Thirty years ago, John Rowe Townsend was writing fierce stories that examined this very slide, and writing them literately, uncompromisingly. According to Jane Langton, cited by Martha V. Parravano writing in *Horn Book* (September–October, 2000, p. 6051), John Rowe Townsend "began the tradition of social realism in British children's literature." For those Americans who haven't read Townsend's fiction until now, this story of how a family is thrust into shattering disequilibrium can be an intriguing introduction to his work.

In an informative afterword that appeared in one edition of the book, John Rowe Townsend says that he originally wondered, "What if some trend we can already see at work in society were to be taken to its logical conclusion?" (189). And he began to think of a family of six. Three years later, he read "about the great German inflation of the 1920s . . . when Germany was in deep depression after its defeat in World War I and tried to solve its problems by printing money" (190). From the confluence of these ideas came the story that can introduce both economic panic and a splendid British writer to American readers.

John Rowe Townsend, born in Leeds in 1922 and educated at Cambridge University, has been known for decades both in Britain and the United States as a writer of, and also about, books for children. Before becoming a full-time author, he was for fourteen years editor of the *Manchester Guardian Weekly* and, overlapping with this, was children's book editor of the *Daily Guardian* for eleven years. His books have received major awards, including the 1970 Boston Globe-Horn Book Award for *The Intruder* and the 1981 Christopher Award for *The Islanders*. He was selected to deliver the May Hill Arbuthnot Honor Lecture in Atlanta in 1971, and gave the Anne Carroll Moore Lecture at the New York Public Library in the same year and the Whittall Lecture at the Library of Congress in 1976. His 1965 book, *Written for Children*, a comprehensive critical study of English-language children's literature from its beginnings to the late twentieth century, reached its sixth American and British editions in 1995.

Noah's Castle was published by Oxford University Press in 1975; J.B. Lippincott brought it to the U.S. in the following year. It appeared in paperback from Penguin Books Ltd. in Peacock, Puffin and Plus imprints from 1978 to 1996. A limited edition came out in 1999 from Green Bay Publications in England. The page numbers used here refer to the Green Bay edition, which is not available in American bookstores.

Virginia Euwer Wolff's books for young readers such as *Make Lemonade,* have all been ALA Notables or ALA Best Books, sometimes both. Each has won prizes and distinctions, including the Jane Addams Peace Award for her softball novel, *Bat 6*, and most recently The National Book Award for *True Believer,* which was also named a Michael L. Printz honor book. She lives and plays the violin in the Pacific Northwest.

Chapter Two

Bobby Marks Redux: Reconsidering Robert Lipsyte's *Summer Rules* and *The Summerboy*

Michael Cart

In his semi-autobiographical novel, *One Fat Summer* (Harper & Row 1977), Robert Lipsyte introduced one of the great characters of young adult literature: brash, obese, wisecracking Bobby Marks. Though often compared with characters from the early work of Philip Roth and Woody Allen, Bobby is very much his own individual person. And his heroic struggle to transform himself by losing forty pounds the summer of his fourteenth year has become essential reading for all concerned with male anxiety about body image and, thanks to intrinsic literary merit, it has also become a modern classic, one of the titles cited by the Margaret A. Edwards Award committee when it selected Lipsyte as the 2001 winner of this prestigious lifetime achievement award.

When, at the end of that fateful summer, Bobby finally succeeds in shedding those famous forty pounds, he bids farewell to his formerly fat self and turns his face to a future full of promise—and challenge—as readers of his next two coming-of-age adventures, *Summer Rules* and *The Summerboy*, discover.

Though not planned as such, these three novels nevertheless comprise an extended *bildungsroman* that captures the essence of American male adolescence in the 1950s. Though rooted in that specific time and abundantly rich in period detail (Lipsyte refers to them as his "historical" novels) (Cart, 73), the books are timeless in their artful incorporation of such themes as self-transformation, the meaning of manhood, sexual awakening, and every teen's urgent need to develop both conscience and social consciousness. To appreciate the full scope of Lipsyte's literary achievement, it is necessary to read all three novels in concert. Yet, sadly, two of the three—*Summer Rules* and *The Summer-*

boy—are now out-of-print, having become, in the process, lost masterworks of young adult literature.

The belated critical acclaim that Lipsyte is now receiving—in addition to the 2001 Edwards Award, he received the 1999 ALAN Award for contributions to young adult literature—offers compelling reason for reissuing these two novels. An equally compelling argument is their continuing thematic relevance to contemporary readers, coupled with their evergreen humor and their richness of characterization and setting.

Summer Rules (Harper & Row 1981) is set in 1954. Two years having passed since his "fat summer," Bobby is now sixteen and dreaming of getting a "real man's job" on a landscape gardening crew (1). His strong-willed, controlling father has a different idea, though. Speaking of the local day camp, he says, "I hear there's an opening at Happy Valley" (1).

Bobby may have lost weight but he hasn't lost his famous sense of humor. Not missing a beat, he cracks, "Better close it quick before all that happiness spills out"(2).

Mr. Marks holds the trump card, however: his promise to teach Bobby to drive. Like most teens, the boy is desperate to get his license and the freedom it represents. He grudgingly accepts the camp job. Mr. Marks keeps his side of the bargain and the ensuing driving lessons become not only a series of funny, rite-of-passage experiences, they also assume metaphoric value in their exposition of the eternal struggle between a father and son for control. "When was I going to be in the driver's seat of my own life?" Bobby wonders (119).

Expanding the book's coming-of-age aspect, Bobby falls in love with a fellow camp employee, green-eyed, hot-tempered Sheila. Through this relationship Bobby will learn a lot about the difference between love and lust while the reader is learning equally important lessons about the historic objectification of women in America.

The relegation of women to a secondary societal role becomes an even more important theme of the third Bobby Marks novel *The Summerboy* (Harper & Row 1982).

It is now the summer after Bobby's freshman year in college, and he has finally secured a real man's job: working at the Lenape Laundry. However, before realizing his long-standing dream of becoming a truck driver (first expressed in *One Fat Summer*), Bobby must endure a brief season in hell, "the soapflake inferno" (46), working inside the plant with the women. It proves to be an epiphanic experience, however, instilling in Bobby new respect for his female co-workers and opening his eyes to the casual contempt with which they are viewed by the other male employees.

Always a romantic, Bobby falls in love once again—this time with a fiery young woman named Diana—and becomes her ally in an increasingly contentious struggle for employee rights. The introduction of this theme dramatizes Lipsyte's lifelong concern with social issues, which manifested itself in his first young adult novel, *The Contender* (Harper & Row 1967); the story of a black teenager, stuck in a dead-end life, who reinvents himself through his discovery of boxing.

Bobby's emerging social conscience is only one of many resemblances to his creator. Another is his desire to become a writer, an ambition that is a leit motif in all three novels. As for Lipsyte, he acknowledges, "the only thing I ever wanted to be was a writer" (Cart, 16).

In realizing his dream, Lipsyte has balanced his career in young adult literature with a working life as a celebrated sports reporter and columnist that began in 1957 when the *New York Times* hired him as a copy boy. "Journalism feeds the fiction," he says, explaining, "it gets me out of the house, introduces me to people and ideas I could never imagine, gives me a license to pry" (Meiners, 1). It also has cultivated a habit of closely observing the world around him, a habit that surely explains the verisimilitude that is such a richly rewarding aspect of the Bobby Marks novels and, indeed, of all the author's young adult work.

The business of journalism is retelling the truth, and so it is no surprise that truth is another of the timeless themes that informs the Bobby Marks trilogy. Indeed, the title *Summer Rules* is a reference to Mr. Marks's passionate belief that no one should take a holiday from truth telling. "Lying is never justified," he sternly tells his son (*Summer Rules,* 85). Though equivocal at first, Bobby will come to embrace this point of view, even though it costs him his job and his relationship with Sheila. It is, the reader understands, the price of integrity, of becoming a responsible adult.

And, indeed, in one of the first scenes in *The Summerboy,* the most adult of the three novels, Bobby tells his prospective employer, "I wouldn't want to start out by lying" (5). However, this does not stop him from continuing to enjoy a rich fantasy life, fuelled by the would-be writer's imagination that he calls his "dream machine" (*Rules*, 70) and further fed by his passionate love for movies and his actor heroes Humphrey Bogart and Alan Ladd.

Circumstances will ultimately drive home the difference between the kind of fantasy heroism he has witnessed on screen and the grittier kind that real life requires. It is a painful lesson. "No wonder you're such a meatball," Bobby tells himself bitterly, "you get all your ideas from movies" (134). Nevertheless in the final scene of the book he cannot resist imagining the words "The End" superimposed on his back as he turns away from the laundry, his work there done and his personal journey from one fat summer to a new season of manhood completed.

If Bobby is now prepared to say "good-bye" to all that, Lipsyte was more reluctant to move away from a literary neighborhood inhabited by characters he had come to think of as his personal repertory company. He toyed with the idea of writing a fourth novel in which he would take Bobby into the Army at the end of the fifties. "I was going to put him into a reserve group and then I would have ended it with his being a summer copy boy at the (New York) *Times*" (Cart, 75).

This never happened, but since, as a writer, Lipsyte resides close to the intersection of real life and art, he couldn't resist bringing his alter ego back for an encore appearance as a minor adult character in his novel *The Chief* (HarperCollins 1993). Now "Professor" Marks, Bobby is head of a university's writing program. Lipsyte himself, of course, has taught writing at both Fairleigh Dickinson and New York University.

Just as Bobby has continued to live inside the head of his creator, so he continues to live inside the minds of generations of young readers, who, inspired by his example, have been challenged to examine the nature of truth, to transform themselves into something better than they might have imagined they could become, to cultivate conscience and social consciousness. Bobby Marks remains one of the truly great characters of young adult literature. Surely it is time for the publisher of those two indispensable stories about him—*Summer Rules* and *The Summerboy*—to transform "lost" into once again "found" masterworks of young adult literature.

BIBLIOGRAPHY

Cart, Michael. *Presenting Robert Lipsyte.* New York: Twayne Publishers, 1995.
Lipsyte, Robert. *The Chief.* New York: HarperCollins, 1993.
———. *The Contender.* New York: Harper & Row, 1967.

Meiners, William. "A Round with Robert Lipsyte." *Sport Literature,* issue 12. Online at www.sportliterate.org/2000_12/lips12.htm) Accessed July 3, 2001.
The Bobby Marks Books:
Lipsyte, Robert. *One Fat Summer.* Harper & Row, 1977.
——. *Summer Rules.* New York: Harper & Row ("An Ursula Nordstrom Book"), 1981.
——. *The Summerboy.* New York: Harper & Row ("A Charlotte Zolotow Book"), 1982.

Recipient of the year 2000 Grolier Award, **Michael Cart** is former director of the Beverly Hills (CA) Public Library and past president of the Young Adult Library Services Association. A nationally known expert in young adult literature, Michael writes the monthly "Carte Blanche" column for *Booklist* and is the author of six books, including *Presenting Robert Lipsyte* (Twayne 1996).

Chapter Three

Welcome Back, Smith! Four Leon Garfield Masterpieces
Katherine Paterson

First published in *The Horn Book Magazine*, January/February 2001.

"He was called Smith and was twelve years old. Which, in itself, was a marvel; for it seemed as if the small pox, the consumption, brain-fever and even the hangman's rope had given him a wide berth for fear of catching something. Or else they weren't quick enough."

Smith is back. In a world where the giant share of news is bad, the news that Leon Garfield's bad boy is alive and well and eager to pick your pocket is good indeed. And Harris is not forgotten! Though who could forget Harris who determines to expose his infant sister to see if "a vixen with full dugs" will adopt her and raise her in the wild? Then there are those caught up in villainy not by choice but by circumstance—Tolly under the power of the not-quite-hanged Black Jack and William who hears footsteps that lead him finally to the mysterious Jack Diamond. They are all back thanks to the publishing wisdom of Farrar Straus Giroux, who are reissuing four of Leon Garfield's masterpieces for a new generation of readers. *Smith* and *Black Jack* appeared in fall 2000, and *John Diamond* and *The Strange Affair of Adelaide Harris* in early 2001.

As an extravagant admirer for more than twenty-five years, it is hard for me to believe that Leon Garfield needs any introduction, but the sad fact is that he must. His books have been allowed to go out of print, so that means that there are too many potential readers out there who have yet to taste the pleasure of a Garfield adventure. How could the work of a writer like Garfield be allowed to go out of print while thousands of mediocre volumes flourish? Garfield himself in a November/December 1988 *Horn Book* article compared certain publishers (which he generously depicted as "mostly British") as being like the current prime minister—more concerned with "minding the store than storing the mind" (736).

> Although telling stories of the past is the oldest form of storytelling, it is regarded by those publishers as being something of an embarrassment, like an elderly relative—to be tolerated out of a sense of duty and reluctantly supported in a condition of genteel poverty. Younger readers don't like historical fiction, publishers say. Six months ago my daughter didn't like asparagus; but now she holds it in such high esteem that she even shares it with her hamster. Young readers find historical fiction difficult, publishers say. When an infant first comes into the world, it finds breathing difficult, but with a little assistance, breathing becomes the most natural thing imaginable. Young readers don't find historical fiction true to life like things on television, publishers say. There's no answer to that one. The writing of historical fiction demands precision, care, and regard for language utterly remote from the cynical incompetence of most television writers." (736–7)

The article cited is a defense of historical fiction. Garfield's books, however, are not your usual sort of historical fiction. They are not concerned with the making or unmaking of nations. Some writers, says Garfield in that same article, "tell tales of great deeds, of battles and kings. Others, like myself, prefer something in a more humble way" (742).

In pursuing his "more humble way," Leon Garfield has often been compared to Charles Dickens. Well, yes, he is like Dickens—or like Dickens might have been with a good editor. The setting of the novels, the picaresque cast of characters, the intricate plotting, the wealth of humor do call Dickens to mind, but Garfield doesn't waste a word in his pursuit of a rollicking tale. His "precision, care and regard for language" is always evident and often twists into delight. After Bostock, Harris's hapless accomplice in *The Strange Affair of Adelaide Harris*, gives the poorhouse matron two shillings to make sure she's drunk and off duty so the two boys can re-abduct Harris's little sister, the matron declares: "'Bless my soul! . . . Another little Christian.' 'No, I ain't,' said Bostock sadly. 'I'm a hypocrite, Mrs. Bonney.' 'I don't care what domination you may be, Master B.,' said Mrs. Bonney. 'You're a real Christian to me.'"

Although, in Garfield's view, publishers were demanding books that were, like television (!), "true to life," what they were and often still are demanding is books that are so superficially like the everyday lives of the intended audience that children will be able effortlessly to "identify" with the characters—books, in short, that will demand no exercise of the imagination.

But if there is to be any hope for the future of the world, then children must be encouraged and enabled to develop their imaginations. How else can they come to understand themselves and others? "Things familiar," as Garfield says, "become invisible, and it is only when we move them to another place or another time that their qualities leap out at us" (op. cit., 741).

William Jones in *John Diamond* is the loving son of a troubled father—as many children today are—but there the superficial resemblance ends. William journeys alone into eighteenth century London, where he falls in with a money-grubbing dwarf and various unsavory characters bent on larceny or vengeance. It is William's determination not only to escape the cruel uncle who has become his guardian, but his determination to atone for his dead father's sin and bring peace to his spirit that thrusts the twelve-year-old into his harrowing London adventure. Yet what child hasn't felt the need to comfort an unhappy parent? What child hasn't longed to run away from a tyrannical adult? Surely most will understand the emotions that impel William on his quest and cheer when it climaxes in William's heroic act that ends a generation of remorse on one side and hatred on the other. It is largely through books, Garfield contends, that persons get to know themselves and others. For, he says, in the March/April 1990 *Horn Book*,

> [a person] is not born with self-knowledge, only with self-awareness. Self-knowledge may be acquired through experience, but that is a very chancy business. It is the rare soul who actually profits by experience. Most of us just keep up with the payments. But self-knowledge can be acquired through art. (168)

Although *The Strange Affair of Adelaide Harris* surely wins the prize for the most hilarious pretzel of a plot in children's books, the other three volumes, while abounding in humor and certainly exemplary in plot construction, show more clearly Garfield's ability to combine those elements in characters that tear at the heart.

In the Carnegie Medal Honor Book, *Black Jack*, the innocent Tolly finds himself the unwilling deliverer not only of a gallows escapee but of a girl being transported to an insane asylum. Much to Tolly's despair, both the criminal and the mad girl come to adore him, laying burdens on the tender-hearted boy that send all three dashing down a path towards tragedy. A child, or any feeling reader, will begin with Tolly's fear and follow him through the heavy weight of responsibility for the two he has rescued into the dawning of affection and the anguish of loss.

Garfield spoke of himself not so much as a writer for children as one that wrote "that old-fashioned thing the family novel, accessible to the twelve-year-old and readable by his elders" (HB oct.74, 38). Now that J. K. Rowling has turned that old-fashioned thing into an international rage, the world may be at last ready for Leon Garfield.

"One does not write for children," he says. "One writes so that children can understand. Which means writing as clearly, vividly, and truthfully as possible" (*Horn Book* Dec. 1968, 671). Surely no better examples of this dictum can be found than Garfield's own books. Take this chilling scene from *Smith,* for a prime example:

> They moved very neat, and with no commotion. They were proficient in their trade. The taller came at the old man from the front; the other took on his back—and slid a knife into it.
>
> The old gentleman's face was fatefully towards a certain dark doorway. He seemed to peer very anxiously round the heavy shoulder of the man who was holding him—as if for a better view. His eyes flickered with pain at the knife's quick prick. Then he looked surprised—amazed, even—as he felt the cold blade slip into his warm heart.
>
> "Oh! Oh! Oh my—" he murmured, gave a long sigh—and died. His last sight on this earth had been of a small, wild and despairing face whose flooded eyes shone out of the shadows with all the dread and pity they were capable of. (7)

In 1987 *Smith*, which twenty years earlier had been an honor book for the Boston Globe-Horn Book, won the prestigious Phoenix Award. The Children's Literature Association gives this award for a book published twenty years earlier that did not at its publication win a major award but which has stood the test of time. The Association is made up largely of English professors who teach children's literature as literature in their respective departments. Such an award must have gratified Garfield who argued eloquently for literature as "a continuous matter, from childhood onward" rather than as "divided into a negligible junior field, and a senior field that is alone worth considering seriously." Children's books, he said, create readers for all books. "A nursery is not an unimportant part of the house" (*Times Literary Supplement*, August 7, 1970 quoted in the *Horn Book* Feb. 1971, 15).

Garfield, who died too soon in 1996, has left a wonderful legacy, and we are all in Farrar Straus Giroux's debt for reissuing these four treasures for readers old and new. But Garfield also left vital instructions for those who seek to write for the young. "Words must live for them," he reminds us. "That is what really matters, and it entails believing entirely in what one writes and having a real urgency to convince the reader that it is absolutely, utterly true." And what for Garfield, whose respect for young readers was evident in every word, made a book a book for children?

Gulliver's Travels (he notes in *Horn Book* Dec. 1968) may be read by the young while *1984* is not suitable. Both are satires; both are fantasies; yet Swift has a sense of wonder . . . and Orwell has only bitterness.

> Is it then, that a young reader requires optimism in one way or another and is bored or repelled by the lack of it? It is tempting to think that that is all there is; but optimism is not enough. There should also be a sense of wonder and a deep belief that, to the spirit, the possible is more important than the probable. (672)

The resemblance between illustrators and their illustrations has often been noted. Less has been said about the kinship between authors and their characters. Leon Garfield, to those who knew him even slightly, was the essence of the British gentleman, courtly and considerate. But by his own words he betrayed the Smith within. Indeed, he argued that we must all cultivate the outlaw within ourselves:

> What I look for in a book that I would want a child to read is that spark of vitality, that glint of indignation, that is the mark of the outlaw within, aiming his inky arrows at injustice and bad authority that will prick the young reader and stir him up into looking at the world about him and saying, "Lord, what fools these mortals be!'" (Dec. 1968, 170)

Garfield has given us just such books—written clearly, vividly, truthfully and with great regard for language. But it is their outlaw quality that will both draw the young reader into the tale and, just possibly, impel him or her to new understandings of self, others, and the hypocrisy of the status quo. Welcome back, Smith. May you live forever.

Katherine Paterson is the author of more than twenty-five books, including thirteen novels for young people, and has twice won both the Newbery Medal and the National Book Award. She is the 1998 recipient of the most distinguished international award for children's literature, the Hans Christian Andersen Medal.

Chapter Four

A Southern Voice Recalled: Two Novels by Mildred Lee

Sue Ellen Bridgers

"You're going to love this book!" It was 1980 and Gail at the county library was handing me a brand new hardback. A glance at the cover showed me a bleak background with two faces, a blond young woman and a bearded young man, peering out of the darkness. The title was *The People Therein*, obviously a Biblical reference I could not identify, and the writer was Mildred Lee, also unknown to me.

"An Appalachian story?" I asked, because Gail knew of my special interest in fiction set in the southern Appalachians of North Carolina where my family and I had come to live in 1971. My subject matter had always been the flat tobacco country of eastern North Carolina, the place of my childhood and a landscape I knew and felt intimately. I was yet to write my first story set in the mountains. To write about a place, one must claim some sort of ownership. How long would that take? I wondered. And what are the requirements?

I brought *The People Therein* home and that evening turned to the notes on the author to discover she lived in Florida. Since western North Carolina has provided respite from mosquitoes and summer heat for low country folks for two hundred years, I grimaced at the thought of yet another "foreigner" spending a little time with us and then making literary hay of our backward ways and quaint speech. I read on to learn she was the daughter of a Baptist minister, which could quite possibly lead to a pious, self-righteous view of mountain mores. She had spent her childhood in a succession of small Southern towns, from my perspective the only mark in her favor. So much for Mildred Lee, I thought. But Gail had said read, and read I would.

A few days later I was back in the library at Gail's desk. "Any more Mildred Lee?" I asked her. Gail handed me *The Skating Rink,* which I read in one sitting.

Two entirely different books. Two different writing styles. Completely different subject matter. One short; the other long. One directed toward junior high students; the other, for young adult and adult readers. Mildred Lee's two books had one thing in common—they were written by a woman with affection for and understanding of her characters; fine, tightly plotted stories to tell; the ability to adapt her considerable gifts to the subject at hand; and a writing style that made her stories accessible but also rich in language and detail. I had discovered a wonderful writer.

Over the years I have read two more of Mildred Lee's books that would be of interest to the young adult reader: *Fog* and *Sycamore Year.* Both of them are fine books available through used book sources, but my heart remembers the first two I read. There are lingering images, poignant and painful moments that for a writer are either spontaneous creative gifts or hard to come by. Either way, in the end the reader has the delight of wonderful stories powerfully told.

In *The Skating Rink,* Mildred Lee tells the story of Tuck Farraday, a fifteen-year-old boy whose stammer has isolated him from both the world and his family. Tuck walks miles from his south Georgia farm to school to avoid being taunted on the bus and intends to quit school altogether when he is sixteen. He does his school and farm work in silence until a roller skating rink starts going up down the road from his house and he meets the owner Pete Degley, who doesn't seem to notice Tuck's stuttering. His growing friendship with Pete gives Tuck reason to feel differently about himself, and so when Pete wants to teach him to skate, Tuck overcomes his embarrassment, begins to work tirelessly at learning to skate and ends up performing a duet with Pete's beautiful young wife at the opening of the skating rink. Along the way, Tuck's speech improves, and he begins to see his father, with whom he has had a particularly strained relationship, in a new, more sympathetic light.

Published in 1969 by Seabury Press, *The Skating Rink* resulted in Mildred Lee receiving the first literary award given to a writer of children's books by the Alabama Library Association. The German language edition received the Austrian National Book Award for Children's Literature in 1971. *Library Journal* called it a "sympathetic account of the difficult interior journey from youth to manhood" and noted that "[Miss Lee] portrays imperfect, troubled, believable people, and her touch in the romantic scenes, so devastating to Tuck, is both realistic and sensitive" (1798). A reviewer at Amazon.com writes, "In a strange twist of fate, I read this book as a youth and I found myself living life in similar circumstances . . . the important thing to know is that you can transcend life's difficulties if you simply begin to believe in yourself!" Produced by ABC as a television "After School Special," the movie version of *The Skating Rink* won a Christopher Award in 1975. The film is currently available through New Kid Home Video.

At least one of Tuck's experiences: his alienation from his family; his isolation at school; his sexual longings and fears; his discovery of himself through a confidence-building endeavor will be familiar to junior high school boys. Girls will respond to Tuck's struggles with peers and family and will appreciate his thoughtful, gentle nature. At a time when we are looking for meaningful stories about boys, stories without graphic sexual encounters or violence, *The Skating Rink* provides a valuable read-aloud or class study novel as well as a fine story to recommend to an individual student. Several writing prompts come to mind: the emotional and physical aspects of a handicap; haunting childhood memories; or a character sketch of a person with whom the reader is in conflict are obvious ones. At 126 pages, this novel is accessible even to reluctant readers.

Eighteen-year-old Ailanthus "Lanthy" Farr, the protagonist of *The People Therein*, lives with her family in the mountains of North Carolina where she is isolated from the rest of the world until a young man from Boston moves into a cabin nearby. The attraction between Lanthy and Drew Thorndike is obvious from their first meeting, and their relationship develops, although Lanthy has a birth defect that has made her feel undesirable, and Drew is well spoken and better educated than anyone else in the valley.

Life in Dewfall Gap will give young adult readers a realistic look at life in turn of the century Appalachia. Lee uses dialect for the native characters, but it is never intrusive and always rings true. Drew, the young Northerner, reveals himself mostly through occasional journal entries and letters to his sister back in Boston, all of which blend smoothly into the flow of the story. Read one and you won't skip the others.

Mildred Lee's descriptive powers are essential to the success of this story, and she uses them effectively, as when she describes the haying:

> First there was the mowing, then the raking and stacking. He did the cutting alone, but Lanthy helped with the raking, glad to be in the meadow rather than the hot house. Soaked in sweat, casting an anxious eye skyward at intervals, she worked as hard as a man. The sweet scent of fresh-mown grass filled the heavy air and at last the cone-shaped stacks stood, fair as a picture in the bottom land separated from the pasture by a rough rail fence. (38)

Here is a picture painted simply, without more detail than the reader needs to construct a vivid image.

In a letter to his sister, Drew Thorndike describes the dancing at a social gathering in Dewfall Gap as lovely and like a complex game he had not expected to see among the mountain people: "circles within circles, hand-clapping, curtseying and bowing as graceful as any I ever saw in a ballroom. The music, a single violin played by a bandy-legged ancient, might have been a full-fledged orchestra" (39). Anyone who has heard fine mountain fiddling would agree with him.

One of the tenets of good writing is selecting the details that give a larger or deeper view than the one actually written. It means letting one detail conjure up many. Whether describing a thunderstorm in the forest, a brush arbor camp meeting or a school Christmas pageant, time and time again Mildred Lee succeeds in portraying a world lost to us.

When I began thinking about this book for young adult readers, I was concerned about the fact that Lanthy has a child in the course of the story. On re-reading, I found the love-making between Lanthy and Drew closer in tone to a romance novel than I had remembered. Still, Drew's commitment to Lanthy and their intention to marry takes precedence over the brief sexual encounters. Even more important is the aftermath of their love-making—Drew leaves suddenly for Boston without knowing Lanthy is pregnant. Lanthy's personal struggles—her relationship with her family, her refusal to name the father of the baby, her doubts about her future—could be, in the hands of a lesser writer, sentimental and maudlin, but Mildred Lee skillfully lifts the plot above the tired strains of the romance novel to finish the story with the characteristic strength and dignity of a mountain woman. Lee's summers in western North Carolina and her deep friendships with people here who were willing to lend her newspaper records and tell stories of past generations provided her with the authenticity apparent in this novel.

First published in 1980 by Houghton Mifflin/Clarion Books, the paperback edition of *The People Therein* was printed by New American Library in 1982. For students who like the Cleaver books and Catherine Marshall's *Christy* or who are already reading John Ehle's wonderful mountain novels, Lee Smith's *Oral History*, or Charles Frazier's *Cold Mountain*, this book would make a fine contribution to their reading pleasure as well as to their knowledge of Appalachian history.

Mildred Lee, now in her nineties, still lives in St. Petersburg, Florida. Her books are a testament to her unaltered faith in the inherent goodness of people and their willingness to struggle to find meaning in the difficulties life brings them. These stories reach beyond the South and the southern Appalachian Mountains. They are universal and spirit-lifting—books to be appreciated by young and old alike.

BIBLIOGRAPHY

GaryTomcat, "An inspirational read!" *Amazon.com.* (15 October 1997).
Lee, Mildred. *Fog.* New York: The Seabury Press, 1972.
———. *The People Therein.* New York: The New American Library, 1982.
———. *The Skating Rink.* New York: The Seabury Press, 1969.
———. *Sycamore Year.* New York: Lothrop, Lee & Shepard Co., 1974.
Sandahl, Margaret E. *Library Journal* 15, (April 1969): 1798.

Sue Ellen Bridgers has written seven novels, all set in rural North Carolina. Recently four of her out-of-print titles, *Home Before Dark, All Together Now, Permanent Connections*, and *All We Know of Heaven* have been published in paperback by Banks Channel Books. Her other novels include *Notes for Another Life, Sara Will,* and *Keeping Christina*. Bridgers and her family live in Sylva, North Carolina.

Chapter Five

A Gringo Comes of Age in the Southwest: Richard Bradford's *Red Sky at Morning*

Chris Crowe

I paid fifty cents for the paperback copy of Richard Bradford's *Red Sky at Morning* that I salvaged from the stack of discarded books at the local public library. Its cover features actors Richard Thomas and Catherine Burns standing nose to nose in a photo still from the 1971 movie based on the novel. Inside the cover, big name reviewers and authors praise the book: *Philadelphia Inquirer*: "You can't put it down." *The New York Times Book Review*: A "novel of consequence. Very entertaining, very readable, very funny." Harper Lee: "A work of art." And Groucho Marx: "A terribly funny book with some of the richest characters I've read about in some years." The back cover lists the stars from the film in addition to Thomas and Burns: Desi Arnaz, Jr., Richard Crenna, Claire Bloom, Harry Guardino, and others.

Red Sky at Morning was first published by Lippincott in 1968. Pocket Book brought out a paperback edition a year later, and the copy sitting on my desk, Pocket's fourteenth printing, appeared in March 1975. It is one of the best southwestern YA novels ever written. In addition to its fine humor and pathos, it presents a realistic view of a *gringo*'s experience in New Mexico.

Everything about this book suggests its success: more than fourteen printings in its first ten years, a feature film adapted from it, and high praise from reviewers and authors. And my paperback discard is by no means an heirloom. The classic southwestern coming-of-age story (not to be confused with two other novels with the same title, one [2000] by Paul Garrison and another [1991] by Andrea Wyman) is still in print; its most recent edition was published in 1999 by Harperperennial Library.

The story is narrated by seventeen-year-old Joshua Arnold, the bright, ironic, only child of Frank Arnold, a wealthy Alabama shipbuilder, from whom Josh inherited his wit and sense of irony. Frank's fragile wife, Ann Dabney Devereaux Arnold, has claims to the old South aristocracy that are more wishful than real. As the story opens in 1944, Josh and his family are having a farewell dinner at their home in Mobile, Alabama, with Josh's girlfriend and a few family friends. This opening scene uses Josh's wry humor to set the tone for most of the novel:

> [Jimbob Buel] was holding a glass of my father's Tavel rosé, looking at the candlelight through the wine, the perfect Virginia connoisseur. He was probably thinking a seventeen-year-old snot like me was too young to know its virtues.
>
> Well, I do know its virtues, Jimbob boy. Paul and I knocked off a bottle of it just last week, warm, a refined accompaniment to cornbread and beef cracklins.
>
> Courtney Ann Conway squeezed my leg under the table. "Ah bet you'll be sorry, leavin' Mobile with all the pawties and all comin' up." I didn't answer right away. I was figuring how to get Jimbob into the Bankhead Tunnel, and pump a little mustard gas in there. If I could block the exits, and use two pumps, maybe. (1)

Josh's father has joined the Navy, and before reporting for duty, he takes his wife and son to their summer home in Corazón Sagrado, a tiny community in northern New Mexico where they are to live for the duration of the war. Mrs. Arnold protests the "primitive" conditions, especially the dearth of southern aristocrats or other people of consequence with whom she might associate, but Josh welcomes the escape from the South.

When school begins, Josh makes friends with Steenie and Marcia. Like them, he is a *gringo*, an outsider in this predominately Hispanic town, and from Steenie he learns the proper local terminology for ethnic groups: "We only recognize three kinds of people in Sagrado: Anglos, Indians, and Natives. You keep your categories straight and you'll make out all right" (32-33). Steenie then points out a particularly attractive girl and asks Josh to classify her. Josh guesses she's a Creole, and Steenie has to re-explain the complex ethnic divisions:

> "She's a Native. Her name's Viola Lopez. She speaks Spanish and English, and she's a Catholic. Don't ever make the mistake of calling her a

Mexican. Her brother will kill you. Of course, if you call her a Creole she'll get confused as hell and think you mean she's part Negro—that is, part dark-skinned Anglo—and her brother will kill you again. So, think of her as a Native, unless you're comparing her with an Indian. Then she's 'white.' Got it?" (33)

After that, Josh has no trouble keeping his categories straight, but much of the humor and conflict in the novel come from his encounters with "Natives" whose Spanish culture and language dominate the county. Throughout the first part of the novel, Josh has to stay alert to avoid being beaten up by Viola's brother, Chango, and his *pachuko* friends. Later in the story, he periodically manages to frustrate both the principal, Ratoncito, and the sheriff, Chamaco.

In addition to his minor run-ins with local authorities, Josh also has to serve as the mediator between the wise Natives, Amadeo and Excilda Montoya, his father has hired to oversee their home and property and the insensitive *gringos* who inhabit his home: his mother, who numbs herself with sherry to take her mind off her loneliness, and the leech and permanent household guest, Jimbob Buel, who appeared in the Arnold household as soon as Frank Arnold left for the Navy. The Montoyas can barely tolerate the racist, narrow-minded habits of Mrs. Arnold and Jimbob and stay on as family employees out of loyalty to Josh's father.

After chapter four, Josh's father is absent from the novel's main action, but his presence is sustained through his letters to Josh and by the local people who often talk about him. His letters, though laced with good-natured irony, provide Josh with comfort and advice while he endures the neurotic behavior of his mother and Jimbob; the anecdotes about his father told by various Sagrado residents strengthen the affection and admiration Josh has for his dad. Both the letters and the anecdotes have a positive influence on Josh and help move him closer to adulthood.

Red Sky at Morning is both a funny and a moving coming-of-age story. Though Josh is bright and independent, he is burdened by the emotional decline of his mother and his fears for his father's safety. He also comes face to face with a number of harsh social realities: violence, teen pregnancy, racism, poverty, family conflict, and death. Thanks to his friendship with Steenie and Marcia and the distant but firm support of his father, Josh survives and learns from the storms of adolescence. When, at the end of the novel, he receives news of his father's death at sea, he is emotionally mature enough to assume the adult responsibility for himself and his family.

Although best known for its humor, *Red Sky at Morning* has plenty of poignant scenes that balance the story, giving it enough literary depth to prevent it from being merely a comic novel. The first few chapters are pure humor, but they are tempered by Josh's semi-serious conversations with his father that reveal their mutual affection. After a number of comic scenes in Sagrado where Josh is initiated into local culture, the reader is brought back to earth in the very painful scene where Mrs. Arnold, drunk, repeatedly slaps Josh and demands that he apologize for disrespecting her and the deadbeat Jimbob. The humor revs up in the next several pages, but readers are again sobered when Josh sees Viola at a pagan ceremony in La Cima and triggers her fall from grace. Soon, though, readers are laughing again at the antics and banter of Josh, Steenie, and Marcia, but the laughter stops when a telegram arrives announcing the death of Frank Arnold.

After Frank Arnold's death, the novel works to a serious conclusion that is the Yang to its opening chapters' humorous Ying. Many of Frank's friends express their heartfelt condolences and, by doing so, reveal to Josh and the reader the depth of Frank's character. The final scene is just as moving; after settling his family's affairs, Josh enlists in the Navy and must say goodbye to Marcia and to Sagrado, both of whom he has come to love.

My description of the novel's movement from comedy to tragedy may make the story sound like an emotional roller coaster ride, but it's not. Richard Bradford controls his narrative so well that the Ying and Yang of funny and serious move back and forth as naturally as the ups and downs of real life. It's a good literary move because the serious and tragic moments in the story enhance the power of its many hilarious scenes. Bradford's skill in balancing comedy and tragedy combined with his menagerie of interesting and memorable characters make this a terrific novel, one that adults and mature young adults will appreciate.

So, if *Red Sky at Morning* has so much going for it, why was it in the library discard pile and why is it included in a book like this? As good as the novel is, it missed being included with its late 1960s contemporaries, *The Outsiders, The Pigman, The Contender*, and *The Chosen* in the YA literature canon. Because the novel is comparable in style and tone to *The Catcher in the Rye, Catch-22*, and most of Jean Shepherd's novels, some teachers may have considered it "too adult" or too controversial for high school English classes. The story does contain some mature situations and language—material that wouldn't work well in a middle or junior high school—but high school juniors or seniors, the kinds of readers who could handle a book like *The Catcher in the Rye* or *Catch-22,* would certainly love *Red Sky at Morning*. Another reason for its absence from the YA canon may be the general downward move of YA books to the middle school audience; this is definitely not a novel for most seventh, eighth, or ninth graders. Finally, its low YA profile may be the publisher's choice. Despite the fact that it's clearly the coming-of-age story of a seventeen-year-old, the book has never been aggressively marketed as a YA novel. Perhaps its success in the mainstream market satisfied its publishers, convincing them that there would be no significant benefit from pushing the novel in the YA market.

Whatever the reasons for its obscurity in the YA literature world, *Red Sky at Morning* remains a splendid novel, one that older YAs and their teachers will thoroughly enjoy.

BIBLIOGRAPHY

Bradford, Richard. *Red Sky at Morning*. New York: Lippincott, 1968; Pocket Book, 1975.

A former gringo resident of New Mexico, **Chris Crowe** now lives in Utah where he is a professor of English at Brigham Young University. In addition to being the 2002 president of ALAN, he is the editor of the YA Literature column for *English Journal* and is the author of a biography of Mildred D. Taylor (Twayne 1999) and a YA novel, *Mississippi Trial, 1955* (Phyllis Folgelman Books 2002).

Chapter Six

Real Stories, Real Voices: The Lost Works of Janet Bode

Teri S. Lesesne

Nonfiction, the only literary genre defined by what it is not, can easily become dated and outmoded. Today's riveting subjects quickly pass to revert to yesterday's fads. For example, once dozens of books were available on subjects such as friendship bracelets, macramé, and calligraphy. The interests of teens can wane quickly; today's topics may not be as fascinating for the next generation. However, some subjects remain relevant and interesting, generation after generation. Topics that deal with the human condition, such as love and acceptance, loss and tragedy, survival and courage are timeless. These are the subjects explored by Janet Bode in three of her most compelling works: *Hard Time: A Real Life Look at Juvenile Crime and Violence* (Laurel-Leaf, 1996), *The Voices of Rape: Healing the Hurt* (Laurel-Leaf, 1990), and *Trust and Betrayal: Real-Life Stories of Friends and Enemies* (Laurel Leaf, 1995).

Though Janet Bode lost her battle with cancer recently, her works remain a testament to her enormous talent. Bode combined the ethnographic (i.e., interviews) and traditional (i.e., facts and figures), blending the two seamlessly to create books that use many of the techniques of quality fiction writing. Yet, sadly, many of her works are either out of print or difficult to obtain. Though lost, each of these books deserves to find a place in the classroom and an audience among today's adolescents, many of which prefer nonfiction.

THE VOICES OF RAPE: HEALING THE HURT

Bode's interest in this topic stemmed both from her own experiences as a victim of rape and a suggestion from her editor. How does someone manage to deal with such a personal attack? How can someone ask for help? Can anyone who has not been raped understand what the victim feels? This book answers those questions and others. As is the case in most of Bode's books, *The Voices of Rape* is divided into sections. After a brief introduction explaining the genesis of the book, Bode shared the stories of victims and perpetrators of both date and stranger rape. A second section offers information from a social worker, police officials, hospital personnel, and other experts in the field. The final portion of the book provides advice about preventing rape. Bibliographies offer resources and an index.

TRUST AND BETRAYAL: REAL-LIFE STORIES OF FRIENDS AND ENEMIES

How do friendships form? What can you do if no one wants to be your friend? What if your parents do not approve of one of your friends? Bode originally set out to write a book about peer pressure. However, as she began her interviews, she was struck time and again by the common threads of the stories teens related about friends and enemies. Eventually, her focus shifted; the book's focus on relationships served to provide a link for readers to others whose stories seem similar. This collection about making friends and dealing with enemies presents stories from teens. Following each story are responses from other teens who have read the story. Questions about the feelings and actions of the individuals involved in the stories are included. These are intended to spur some discussion among readers.

HARD TIME: A REAL LIFE LOOK AT JUVENILE CRIME AND VIOLENCE

Bode and her partner, Stan Mack, examined the juvenile justice system from the inside out in this selection. The book presents three aspects of juvenile crime and violence. Section I recounts the stories of teens incarcerated for a variety of offenses. Some have committed murder; others are both victims and victimizers. Their stories are told dispassionately. Bode and Mack remained simply scribes, allowing the teens to use their own words. Section II, labeled "Go-Betweens," provides information from juvenile officers, doctors, and researchers. The final section features the voices of teens on the outside whose lives have been touched by crime and violence. Mack, a graphic artist, used a cartoon format to relate some of the stories and other facts included in the book.

One of the greatest qualities of Janet Bode's work was her ability to capture the voice of real teens. Without seeming condescending or judgmental, she allowed teens to speak for themselves. How did Bode manage to get teens to bare their souls to her? How did she inspire the trust that allows them to confide in her? As she suggested in an interview several years ago,

> When kids tell me terrible events of their lives, I act as a kind of reality check. Depending on the circumstances, I might say that what they went through was rotten. No one human being should do to another what happened to them. Or I might praise them for being courageous or inventive for surviving something so threatening."(Lesesne, 1999)

The ability to remain unbiased without being dispassionate was also a hallmark of Bode's work. It was obvious that Bode cared deeply about the subjects she explored in her books. When one reads any of the introductory matter from the books, it becomes clear that Bode had a vested interest in her subject matter. However, while she conducted the interviews, she tried to remain uncritical. Bode instead allowed the voices of the teens themselves and the professionals whose advice was always included to judge and evaluate. Teen readers can quickly see Bode as an ally, someone who truly cared about their thoughts and feelings.

Bode, however, did not simply present the stories of her teen subjects. All of her books offer professional advice to teens who might find themselves in similar circumstances. She provided resources and references for these readers, pointing them to experts in the field or other books on the topics or organizations established to provide help specifically to teens. This advice, from experts in the various fields, adds to the authenticity of the writing. Bode had done her homework. Interviews with teens were only one small part of what went into the production of a book. She said:

> For me researching and writing nonfiction means I get both to go on an adventure and be a detective. I'm in search of the truth about a particular issue. And because I specialize in the human condition, I'm always trying

to find how and why we behave the way we do and what good we can learn from each other. (Lesesne, 1999).

Teens today believe, as did their predecessors, that they are the first youths to experience crime and violence, betrayal by friends, and problems dealing with their peers. One of the real strengths of Bode's work is that it continues to inform today's readers that times are tough for each generation, that others have indeed survived crime, violence, rape, failed relationships, and the like. Helping teens see that their lives today intersect with the lives of teens from other places and other times provides that universality in the reading experience, an experience that can help teens forge connections not only to others like themselves but to those who might be a bit different. The topics explored by Bode in these works and others are classic and timeless. Whether she was writing about peer pressure, violence, fear, friendship, or crime, Bode's books continue to underscore the universality of these themes and topics for readers yesterday, today, and tomorrow.

BIBLIOGRAPHY

Bode, Janet. *Hard Time: A Real Life Look At Juvenile Crime And Violence.* New York: Delacorte, 1996.
——. *Trust And Betrayal: Real Life Stories Of Friends And Enemies.* New York: Laurel Leaf, 1995.
——. *The Voices Of Rape: Healing the Hurt.* New York: Laurel Leaf, 1990.
Carter, Betty, and Richard F. Abrahamson. *From Delight to Wisdom: Nonfiction for Today's Young Adults.* Westport, CT: Oryx Press. OP.
Lesesne, Teri S. "Investigation, Collaboration, And Information: An Interview With Janet Bode And Stan Mack." *Teacher Librarian*, 26. no.3 (February-February 1999).

Teri S. Lesesne is an associate professor of library science at Sam Houston State University in Texas where she teaches courses in literature for young adults. She is past president of ALAN and writes the YA review column for *Voices From the Middle.*

Chapter Seven

Gleeps, or a Case for Trixie Belden

Kathleen Krull

She's fifty-four years old, most frequently described as spunky (also feisty, insatiably curious, impulsive), and has a famous mess of blond curls. Rumors swirl of her own TV show or movie. With ideal casting, she could have been portrayed by a young Hayley Mills, or in today's terms perhaps Reese Witherspoon. Not only did she never marry, but she never "did it" with her love interest, Jim Frayne. Actually she hasn't really done anything since 1986.

But type in her name on a search engine, and you'll get some 2,500 hits. Numerous websites enshrine her, crafted by ardent, even obsessive fans. They point to her similarity to Sue Grafton's Kinsey Millhone, and to her infinite superiority over Nancy Drew. Her adventures are rated "G" and also "C" for collectible—hundreds of editions are selling on e-Bay for many times their cover price. In 1998, a scholarly study on her was presented at the national conference of the Popular Culture Association.

"Gleeps," as Trixie Belden might say, "how perfectly perfect to be a cult figure?!"

Trixie starred in thirty-nine mysteries published by Golden Press/Western Publishing from 1948 to 1986. She lived on Crabapple Farm just outside fictional Sleepyside-on-the-Hudson, New York, with her parents and three brothers. In book 1 she embarks on her first mystery with her new best friend, Honey Wheeler. Someday, the two hope to start the Belden-Wheeler Detective Agency.

A real person wrote the first books in the series—Julie Tatham (1908–1999). She was working as a New York City literary agent when Western put out a call for fast-paced, well-written mystery-adventures to be priced low enough for kids to buy on their own. Western was responding to public pressure to lure kids away from "evil" comic books (many of which, as it happened, Western published). Tatham proposed herself as the writer (using her maiden name of Campbell), came up with the Beldens and Honey Wheeler, and based the setting and details on her own life in the Hudson River Valley. (Other series to which she contributed include Cherry Ames, Vicki Barr, and Ginny Gordon.)

After six books, she was ready to stop, but the publisher wasn't. Campbell received royalties for a while, but eventually all rights reverted to Western. Books 7 to 39 were written under the pseudonym "Kathryn Kenny" by various freelancers hired for flat fees. In the 1970s, editors compiled an elaborate "Trixie Lore" to be used as a bible by the writers. The peak of its popularity was approximately 1979 — when six books were published (23–28), with six more in 1980 (29–34). Trixie sold well, but never achieved quite the heights of Nancy Drew. In one of those publishing Catch-22s, Western's distribution system for older readers was not as effective as it was for the very young. With Little Golden Books selling by the millions, Trixie tended to sink on the list of priorities. The whole series has been out of print for many years — definitely lost (though rumors of revival never die).

For now the Bubbly One lives on through a dedicated fan base, mostly (but not all) women. The biggest fans seem to be in their late twenties to early thirties — women who read the books as teens, never forgot them, and long to share them with their daughters. On websites they treat "our dear Trixie" and other major characters as real people. "I wanted to BE Trixie" is a frequent comment. They write fan letters (sometimes emotional), chat on message boards, plan discussions of individual books, bemoan the end of the series, and circulate petitions to the publisher to reprint. Out of their devotion, they do some serious critiquing and nit-picking, particularly of the Kathryn Kenny titles. They meet up with each other at the 2000 Trixie Belden Convention in White Plains (the nearest real city to Sleepyside) and other fan gatherings around the country.

Most interesting of all, they've taken the series underground, thanks to post-Trixie technology. On the web are dozens of new stories using the beloved characters, often as if they had grown older. The stories are categorized in various ways and range from "wholesome" to "adult" — yes, for some sites you have to prove you're eighteen.

So what is the deal?

Full disclosure: In a past life, while working at Western/Golden Books in Racine, Wisconsin, in the late 1970s, I was an editor on the Trixie series. Several manuscripts required editing to the point of rewriting, and I was emboldened to ask if I could write my own, which I did. (28 is full of Krulls and other clues I could plant as to my identity.) I receive more fan mail on this work than anything else I have written. This year brought the school picture of a Montana girl, with a list of her likes (reading, skating, horses) and three favorite books—all Trixies. When I mention the Blond One in talks, I get squeals from readers of the right age.

I can't make a case for the literary quality of Trixie compared to other titles in this collection of "Masterworks," but the books do seem to have values that remain timeless. They were solid series fiction of the type that people remember fondly for years, and with a bit of brushing off, they could slip back into print fairly easily.

An overall plot for the thirty-nine books might be: just one darn mystery after another. Like life. Trixie exists to puzzle things out, to put clues together, to deduce and infer and sometimes guess, to work through anxieties as her teen world grows more ambiguous. At first she matured and grew up in a normal sequence, but after the first sixteen books (when Western was envisioning many more titles, and decided they'd rather skip certain situations in a rated G series), the editors froze her age at fourteen.

The books are to a large extent plot-driven, but more multi-dimensional than a typical series. The characters are generally well-developed, above all our Sleuthing Queen. She comes across as human and down-to-earth, with the out-of-control hair, pesky brothers, an allowance she has to earn, and a bunch of things she's not good at. Her parents have lots of rules and not enough money. Some of her friends are wealthy and able to bankroll excursions (usually not that exotic—a dude ranch in Arizona, a sheep farm in Iowa, a fishing lodge in the Ozarks), but Trixie always, always has chores. All of the characters have strong work ethics and are responsible citizens without being too dweeby about it.

As a detective, Trixie is never glamorous, but she is believable, more of an Everygirl. She is practical and shrewd (and, it goes without saying, highly intelligent), but she does make mistakes. She jumps to conclusions, rushes into danger, embarrasses herself on a regular basis. And she likes to stay comfortable in her jeans.

The original author, Julie Campbell, considered herself a fervent feminist, and surprisingly little updating would be needed in this area (perhaps give "Moms" a job besides totally clichéd housewife). The heroic acts are almost always performed by girls. Trixie holds her own against two domineering older brothers, a younger brother she has to take care of, a sexist society, and pressure from girls not in her league. With resistance as a way to endure adolescent turmoil, she's always rejecting expectations of her as a typical teen. Repeatedly she demonstrates how to be successful and confident without being pretentious or inhumane. Other characters hoot at and tease Trixie, and it's a real pain when no one takes her seriously as a detective—Sergeant Molinson of the local police force is never glad to see her—but in the end they tend to come around.

It was of primary importance to Campbell that teens should solve their own problems without help from adults—this is a key to Trixie's appeal. Another is the ever-popular notion of the secret, kids-only club. Trixie and her six best friends form the Bob-Whites of the Glen (or BWGs), doing good deeds along with their sleuthing. Friendship is central. The Bob-Whites are generous and respectful teens who care about each other, their families, and their community. They may argue, but they never break their bond.

Each book contains an unusual amount of solid information, most notably on the natural world—especially on the flora and fauna of the Hudson River Valley, as well as its history and folklore. (While researching for book 28, I visited that area for the first time and felt like I knew it well, just from Trixie.)

Incorporated into the mysteries are actual lessons—on medical knowledge, food preparation, American history, numismatics, topics depending on the author's areas of expertise. Books by Campbell and others display a thorough knowledge of horses. Campbell was one of the first American women polo players, and horseback is the preferred mode in Trixieland. Implied throughout is a core value of healthy and sane country living, as embodied by Trixie trying to forge her path in this mysterious world.

The books are not deep, and the writing is not literary—but it is spare, focussed, bubbly, not embarrassing. Banter between the characters is perhaps not quite at the "Buffy, the Vampire Slayer" level, but does become repartee, particularly when brother Mart teases Trixie with arcane words and convoluted sentences.

In "saving" Trixie from being "lost," editing would be necessary to update references and slang, to speed up the pace occasionally in an age when patience for description has waned, to correct stereotypes, to revise various bits that have grown just too corny. These books are for-pleasure reading, not so much as for classroom use, but books kids can afford on their own. Series books can be a great comfort and motivation to young readers—and Trixie Belden seems to deserve another look.

BIBLIOGRAPHY

Keeline, James D. and Kimberlee. "Trixie Belden, Schoolgirl Shamus," a paper presented to the Popular Culture Association, 1998, available online at http://www.keeline.com/Trixie_Belden.pdf

Mason, Bobbie Ann. *The Girl Sleuth: A Feminist Guide*. The Feminist Press, 1975. ("Just Plain Trixie," pages 91–98.)

Listing of Trixie Authors to Date

1. *The Secret of the Mansion* (1948) by Julie Campbell
2. *The Red Trailer Mystery* (1950) by Campbell
3. *The Gatehouse Mystery* (1951) by Campbell
4. *The Mysterious Visitor* (1954) by Campbell
5. *The Mystery Off Glen Road* (1956) by Campbell
6. *The Mystery in Arizona* (1958) by Campbell
7. *The Mysterious Code* (1961) by Nicolete Merideth Stack
8. *The Black Jacket Mystery* (1961) by Stack
9. *The Happy Valley Mystery* (1962) by Stack
10. *The Marshland Mystery* (1962) by Stack
11. *The Mystery at Bob-White Cave* (1963) by Stack
12. *The Mystery of the Blinking Eye* (1963) by Stack
13. *The Mystery on Cobbett's Island* (1964) by Mary Wilkinson
14. *The Mystery of the Emeralds* (1965) by Wilkinson
15. *The Mystery on the Mississippi* (1965) by Stack
16. *The Mystery of the Missing Heiress* (1970) by Stack
17. *The Mystery of the Uninvited Guest* (1977) by Gladys Baker Bond
18. *The Mystery of the Phantom Grasshopper* (1977) by Polly Curren Fedosiuk
19. *The Secret of the Unseen Treasure* (1977) by Carl Henry Rathjen
20. *The Mystery off Old Telegraph Road* (1978) by Laura French
21. *The Mystery of the Castaway Children* (1978) by Bond

22. *The Mystery on Mead's Mountain* (1978) by Donna Walsh Shepherd
23. *The Mystery of the Queen's Necklace* (1979) by Owenita Sanderlin
24. *The Mystery at Saratoga* (1979) by French
25. *The Sasquatch Mystery* (1979) by Bond
26. *The Mystery of the Headless Horseman* (1979) by Joan Chase Bowden
27. *The Mystery of the Ghostly Galleon* (1979) by Bowden
28. *The Hudson River Mystery* (1979) by Kathleen Krull
29. *The Mystery of the Velvet Gown* (1980) by Bowden
30. *The Mystery of the Midnight Marauder* (1980) by Bowden
31. *The Mystery at Maypenny's* (1980) by Bowden
32. *The Mystery of the Whispering Witch* (1980) by Bowden
33. *The Mystery of the Vanishing Victim* (1980) by French
34. *The Mystery of the Missing Millionaire* (1980) by French
35. *The Mystery of the Memorial Day Fire* (1984) by French
36. *The Mystery of the Antique Doll* (1984) by Leslie McGuire Max
37. *The Pet Show Mystery* (1985) by French
38. *The Indian Burial Ground Mystery* (1985) by Max
39. *The Mystery of the Galloping Ghost* (1986) by French

A Few of the Sites from "The Trixie Belden Site Ring"

Trixie Belden Homepage, http://barbln.cygnus.org/trixie.htm
The Trixie Belden FAQBOOK Homepage, The Trixie Belden Library,
    http://trixie.hypermart.net/index.htm
Trixie Belden Tidbits,
    http://www.geocities.com/RainForest/Vines/9158/trixie.html

Kathleen Krull is the author of *Lives of Extraordinary Women: Rulers, Rebels . . . And What the Neighbors Thought* (Harcourt, 2000), other biographies for young readers, and *Trixie Belden and The Hudson River Mystery* (#28). See how nosy she is at www.kathleenkrull.com.

Chapter Eight

The Last Mission by Harry Mazer: Heroism and Hell in World War II
John Noell Moore

Harry Mazer created Jack Raab, the protagonist of *The Last Mission*, from his own experiences in World War II. This powerful novel has been lost to the secondary classroom because, I suspect, teachers continue to teach the standard war novels, like *All Quiet on the Western Front*, or young adult novels about more recent wars, such as Walter Dean Myers's *Fallen Angels*. Mazer's novel deserves a place in our classrooms, and given Tom Brokaw's work in bringing World War II to the forefront of American consciousness, the time seems right to "find" it and teach it.

The autobiographical elements in *The Last Mission* are immediately clear: Mazer dedicates it to the crew with whom he served. He tells their story, from their training to the tragic final mission, which only Jack survives. In flashbacks we learn that fifteen-year-old Jack lied about his age and used his older brother's birth certificate to enlist in the army, that he left home without telling his parents what he was doing, and that he has a romantic interest in college student Dotty Landon.

At the heart of *The Last Mission* is Jack's adolescent dream of becoming a hero; he even imagines himself killing Hitler. However, as a frightened waist gunner in a B-17 bomber, he learns that this "wasn't the war he'd dreamed it would be back home in the Bronx." He'd imagined himself "one of those flying aces ripping around the sky in a fighter plane, shooting down Germans left and right." When he faces reality, he understands that it is "just the war, day after day, like a foot jammed in his belly" (Mazer 83).

Mazer structures the novel in four parts, the first three preceded by a war song of the day. "Part 1: The Crew" opens with "There's a Star-Spangled

Banner Waving Somewhere," its lyrics an appropriate prelude to Jack's heroic fantasies. In "Part 2: The Missions" the imagery of the Army Air Corps' song predicts aerial success (fame) or failure (flame). Here we follow the crew through twenty-four missions, each one so terrifying that Jack never fires his gun. In "Part 3: Bail Out," "Comin' in on a Wing and a Prayer" foreshadows the fatal mission over Czechoslovakia, Jack's parachuting from the falling plane, his capture as a POW, and his release. In "Part 4: Home" Jack returns to his family, to Dotty, and to hard-nosed Army officials who finally discharge him honorably.

With the novel, readers have an opportunity to study how Mazer develops Jack's interior world and how Jack's war experiences destroy his heroic idealism. In the early chapters Mazer juxtaposes Jack's experiences and thoughts by setting his fantasies in italics. Jack daydreams of protecting his Jewish family from German soldiers (11) and of leading *"Raab's band of Jewish volunteers, mere boys, but all with hearts like lions"* into Nazi territory (13). He fantasizes piloting a P-51 Mustang and blowing a German Messerschmitt ME 109 from the sky, about returning home a hero (25) and about his post-war career as an innovative but aloof architect (38).

Mazer balances these early dreams with Jack's nightmare visions following the last mission. Hiding to escape German capture, he re-lives his best friend Chuckie's death (116), and flashbacks of the same scene haunt him as a POW (127). When a clerk at Squadron Headquarters in England reports to him on his crew, Jack thinks, *"Fuckin' squad-room commandos, fighting the war on their asses . . . talk, that's all they know how to do."* The report is *"just a lot of fuckin' words"* (159). Looking at photographs he thinks, *"You're alive, they're dead"* (160). Suddenly he remembers the opening words of the Air Corps anthem, and Mazer dissolves Jack's heroic dreams: "All those beautiful lies about soldiers, and war, and boys in battle" (160). The memory of the last mission shatters the heroic ideal forever.

After he decides to go back to high school, Jack speaks at a Veteran's Day assembly. "War," he says, is "one stupid thing after another": "War isn't like the movies. It's not fun and songs. It's not about heroes" (188). After his speech Jack hears little of the applause about which he once dreamed because he is living in the horror of memory: "The floor of the radio room was still slippery with Chuckie's blood. . . . Dave was still fumbling with his chute . . . and the plane was still falling through the sky" (188). The war replays in his mind in the present tense, and Mazer suggests that it will replay there again and again.

The Last Mission by Harry Mazer

The Last Mission presents a vivid picture of World War II and the culture that Tom Brokaw celebrates in *The Greatest Generation* (1998), *The Greatest Generation Speaks: Letters and Reflections* (1999), and *An Album of Memories: Personal Histories from the Greatest Generation* (2001). These books complement Mazer's novel by elaborating the historical context but also by giving students glimpses into the lives of men and women like those who inhabit Mazer's fictional world. The concept of the hero has changed since World War II, Brokaw observes: "'Hero' is a description tossed around lightly these days—like 'star' or 'celebrity.'" During the war, however, "the phrase 'You're a hero' was likely to bring on the quick rejoinder, 'No, I'm not; I'm just doing my job here—like everyone else'" (1998, 103). Like Brokaw's greatest generation, Jack returns home with a new concept of collective heroism and with "fundamental lessons in the random nature of mortality" (1999, 222) learned in a time of "deprivation and war, heroism and belief, uncertainty and peril" (2001, ix).

Brokaw's *Album* contains a history that uncannily resembles Jack's. While escorting B-17 bombers to Berlin, Lester Varnall was shot down and captured, interrogated by the Gestapo, and imprisoned as a POW before he finally escaped to an American camp. His words could come straight from Jack's lips: "Scared!!!! Damn right I was scared, and any person who has faced combat and tells you he was not scared is lying.... I was terrified but went forward because the rest of the company went forward" (2001, 105). Many young people today seem to have little sense of what it means to depend so heavily and thoroughly on others for safety and security. Many of them believe that they can have it all, that they can do it their way, that each of them is the center of the universe, and that the culture is obliged to hand them a future and ensure their success.

In addition to the Brokaw texts, *The Last Mission* can be used as a source for cultural study. Teachers and students can explore other texts that the novel suggests: the war songs; the film *North Star*; and the war posters of the era. The novel can be put in conversation with other war novels (*The Red Badge of Courage*; *All Quiet on the Western Front*) and with poems about the disillusionment of war (Randall Jarrell's "The Death of the Ball Turret Gunner"; Sigfried Sassoon's "Suicide in the Trenches"). Other World War II young adult novels can enrich and be enriched by Mazer's text: *Under the Blood Red Sun* (Salisbury), *Jacob Have I Loved* (Paterson), and *The Journal of Scott Pendleton Collins: A World War II Soldier* (Myers).

Mazer's *A Boy at War: A Novel of Pearl Harbor* (2001) complements *The Last Mission* in its story of Adam Pelko and his navy family stationed in Hawaii. Similarities exist: Like Jack, Adam's father lied about his age to join the navy, and like Jack, Adam, who is fascinated by fighter planes, romanticizes the war. The novel's undercurrent of racism against Americans of Japanese ancestry (AJAs) is the subject of a detailed "Author's Note" at the end of the novel.

The Last Mission and *A Boy at War* can raise the social consciousness of today's youth. Brokaw says that while we face no world war and no Great Depression, "racial discrimination remains an American cancer" and "economic opportunity is an unending challenge." Most importantly, we "need to reinstate the concept of common welfare in America" because "World War II and what came after was the result of a nation united, not a nation divided" (1998, 388-89).

Both of Mazer's World War II novels play out the archetypal young adult theme: the awakening of the innocent adolescent to the brutal realities of adulthood. The lesson Mazer conveys is aptly stated in the epigraph to *A Boy at War*, a quotation from Samuel Hynes' *Flights of Passage: Reflections of a WW II Aviator*: "Nobody, however young, returns from war still a boy" (vii). Mazer helps us teach this lesson through literature, and let us hope that future generations of students will be able to learn it only from books such as *The Last Mission*.

BIBLIOGRAPHY

Brokaw, Tom. *The Greatest Generation*. New York: Random House, 1998.
———. *The Greatest Generation Speaks: Letters and Reflections*. New York: Random House, 1999.
———. *An Album of Memories: Personal Histories from The Greatest Generation*. New York: Random House, 2001.
Crane, Stephen. *The Red Badge of Courage*. New York: Norton, 1982.
Jarrell, Randall. "The Death of the Ball Turret Gunner." In *The Top 500 Poems*, ed. William Harmon. New York: Columbia University Press, 1992. 1047.
Mazer, Harry. *A Boy at War: A Novel of Pearl Harbor*. New York: Simon and Schuster, 2001.
———. *The Last Mission*. New York: Bantam Doubleday Dell, 1979.
Myers, Walter Dean. *Fallen Angels*. New York: Scholastic, 1988.
———. *The Journal of Scott Pendleton Collins: A World War II Soldier*. New York: Scholastic, 1999.

Paterson, Katherine. *Jacob Have I Loved*. New York: HarperTrophy, 1980.
Remarque, Erich Maria. *All Quiet on the Western Front*. Trans. A.W. Wheen. Reprint. New York: Little, Brown, 1929.
Salisbury, Graham. *Under the Blood-Red Sun*. New York: Bantam Doubleday Dell, 1984.
Sassoon, Sigfried. "Suicide in the Trenches." 634. in *England in Literature (Macbeth Edition)*. Glenview: IL: Scott, Foresman and Company, 1973.

A former secondary English teacher, now professor of English education at William and Mary, **John Noell Moore** is the author of *Interpreting Young Adult Literature: Literary Theory in the Secondary Classroom*. He has served on the ALAN Board of Directors and edits regular columns for *The ALAN Review* and *English Journal*.

Chapter Nine

Sex Education by Jenny Davis: Lessons in Caring and Healing
Ann Wilder

I first encountered *Sex Education* in February of 1989 when I was searching for a book to read aloud to my students. As I read it, I suspected right away that it would be a successful book to read to these ninth and tenth graders. First of all, there is the first-person narrator. (My students are crazy about books with first-person narrators.) Then there is the initial mystery. Why, the reader wants to know, is Livvie in the mental institution? Then there's the romance between Livvie and David. And, there's the high school setting and the topic of sex.

Part of our daily routine in my English classes is for me to begin class by reading aloud from a young adult novel. I read aloud for five to ten minutes at the beginning of each class period; the students actively listen. This means they do not finish up last minute homework assignments, they do not sneak a quick nap, nor do they talk to each other. My part of the bargain is that I find books they will enjoy listening to. In addition, the students know that there will be no worksheets, vocabulary lists, or tests on the books they hear read aloud. What there will be is discussion on the book and perhaps a written reflection or response at key points in the reading.

When I choose books to read to my students or books to teach as class novels, I always look for books that the students will enjoy, but I also select books for my own "teacher reasons." What appealed to me, as a teacher, about *Sex Education* was the concept of the sex education class taught by Mrs. Fuller. This teacher is passionate about her subject matter, and her students clearly love the class. As a teacher I enjoyed watching her in action. The reader in me quickly became fond of the character Livvie as she describes her relationship with David and the chain of events leading up to David's death. Even though she is telling her story a year after the events have occurred, her narrative voice still contains some of the innocence that the horror of her experience could not remove.

When the novel opens, Livvie explains that she is a patient in the University Psychiatric Institute and that she has been there for a year. She introduces her narrative by saying that her psychiatrist has instructed her to write down her story as a part of the healing process. Livvie begins her story with the first day of her freshman year of high school, the day she meets David Kindler in her biology class. Mrs. Fuller, their biology teacher, explains to her students on the first day of class that she has worked over the summer at the local health department where she has learned first-hand about the numbers and effects of teen pregnancies. She has decided to supplement the biology curriculum by expanding the unit on birth control to include specific information on human reproduction. Additionally, she introduces her students to the concept of caring—caring for themselves and caring for others.

The culminating project for students in Mrs. Fuller's class is a caring project in which students select a person to care about. Livvie and David decide to work together on the project and settle on new neighbors, the Parkers, to use as subjects for their project. Mrs. Parker—Maggie—is in the early stages of pregnancy and seems needy. Maggie's husband Dean is unfriendly to the point of putting up signs around his house warning people to keep out. Dean even tells them, in one of their visits, to "stay the hell away" from his house. Livvie and David concentrate on caring for Maggie and are careful to visit her only when Dean is at work. As they become involved with Maggie and share her lonely, frightened world, their own relationship deepens. The horror of Maggie's world becomes real to Livvie and David when they see the bruises on Maggie's body. As they attempt to take Maggie and her new baby from her home, the husband arrives and pushes David, causing him to lose his footing on an icy front step and fall to his death, sending Livvie into a world of silence.

I would like to see this book return to print and into the hands of high school students. The teenagers in my classroom love the story. They admit that the provocative title draws them in but then the characters and plot hook them. The teen characters—Livvie, David, and their biology classmates—are real. Livvie has all the familiar teenage characteristics: She doesn't believe she is pretty; her parents embarrass her; and she worries about what others think and say about her. The students in the biology class also ring true as they groan and roll their eyes when Mrs. Fuller lectures them on abstaining from sex.

Sex Education is rich with ideas for discussion. Mrs. Fuller presents the problem of teen pregnancy as a rationale for the addition of the sex education unit to her biology curriculum. But her message, that teens (and everyone else, for that matter) should *care* about another person before they have sex, is clear. In fact, David and Livvie, after several months of sex education and after six months of their own relationship, realize that caring for each other has led them to decide to have sex. Even though they plan to contact Planned Parenthood and their health department first, some of my students question the effectiveness of the sex education class. Lively discussion ensues.

Another issue in the book is that of spousal abuse. David and Livvie know that things are not right with Maggie and Dean Parker—that something is terribly wrong in that house. Maggie appears after Christmas with a broken arm; she explains the injury by saying that it was her fault. After her baby is born, Livvie and David find Maggie horribly bruised, but Maggie denies that Dean is beating her and again tells them that it is her fault. The tragedy comes in the fact that they do not tell anyone about how bad things actually are in the house *and* in the fact that the adults in whom they do confide some of their suspicions— David's mother and Mrs. Fuller—do not become more active. At the end of the book, Mrs. Fuller visits Livvie in the sanitarium where she has lived for almost a year and confesses to Livvie that she feels responsible for David's death. Her teacher's confession actually helps Livvie begin to heal and want to start living again.

Sex Education offers teachers an opportunity to work collaboratively with the school nurse or health teacher to discuss with their students issues surrounding sexual issues for teens. As a culminating project, students research current statistics on teen pregnancy and sexually transmitted diseases. In addition, tapping community resources such as a community agency that works with battered women provides students with information on some of the steps that Maggie Parker could have taken to improve her situation.

For the English teacher *Sex Education* is extremely teachable as a novel. It is rich in elements of literature and can be used in teaching foreshadowing, theme, and character development. Examples of foreshadowing abound in the novel. The Prologue makes us aware that

Livvie has suffered some horrible tragedy. We have clues that someone will fall from the Parkers' front steps from the first time David and Livvie visit Maggie—and on other visits as well—we notice that the steps leading up to the Parkers' porch are very steep. Themes in the novel also provide ample opportunities for discussion. My students found it interesting to talk about the positive and negative implications of caring. David and Livvie cared for the Parkers and the results were David's death and Livvie's stay in the Psychiatric Institute. Many of my students support David and Livvie's actions, but others believe that caring would mean respecting the Parkers' privacy.

I can only speculate why *Sex Education* has been lost to today's teens, and I suspect that it just didn't sell enough copies to remain in print. I find it interesting that *Say Goodnight, Gracie*, another novel dealing with death and healing and one that was published within a year of *Sex Education* continues to be popular with teenagers. *Sex Education* is, however, still available in libraries and serves as a good companion book to more recent young adult novels dealing with issues of abuse, loss, and healing. In *Dreamland*, by Sarah Dessen, Caitlin's boyfriend physically abuses her, and she hides signs of the abuse from her family and friends. Finally Caitlin's parents step in and help her begin the healing process. *Speak*'s Melinda spends her ninth grade year suffering the effects of a horrible trauma and withdraws completely from friends and family. Students who enjoy *Say Goodnight, Gracie, Dreamland*, and *Speak* would also find *Sex Education* a satisfying read. Teachers who decide to share *Sex Education* with their students by reading it aloud to them will enjoy the experience of a good story shared and will keep this book alive for teenagers.

BIBLIOGRAPHY

Anderson, Laurie Halse. *Speak*. New York: Farrar Straus & Giroux, 1999.
Davis, Jenny. *Sex Education*. New York: Dell, 1988.
Deaver, Julie Reece. *Say Goodnight, Gracie*. New York: HarperTrophy, 1989.
Dessen, Sarah. *Dreamland*. New York: Viking Children's Books, 2000.

Ann Wilder is a former teacher at Southern High School in Durham, North Carolina, where she taught freshman and sophomore English as well as young adult literature and mass communications. She currently reads and writes about young adult literature and works as a consultant in the field of English/language arts.

Chapter Ten

Opening Up: *The Secret Diary of Adrian Mole Aged 13¾* by Sue Townsend

Alleen Pace Nilsen

The Secret Diary of Adrian Mole Aged 13¾ by Sue Townsend is now more than twenty years old, if we start counting with its initial publication in London, rather than its 1986 American debut. It is a wonderful book to have in a classroom library for eighth, ninth, and tenth graders because once a single student has read it, chances are that it will be passed from friend to friend. For an introductory booktalk to get that first reader hooked, you might say something like this:

> Adrian Mole is a boy most of you will enjoy getting to know through *The Secret Diary of Adrian Mole aged 13¾*. Author Sue Townsend is a British comic writer of plays for radio, television, and the stage, which has given her lots of practice in recreating people's speech. In Adrian's daily diary, which he starts on January 1, readers get the feeling that Adrian is talking directly to them when on Tuesday, January 20, he frets about his mother looking for a job:
>
> "Now I could end up a delinquent roaming the streets and all that. And what will I do during the holidays? I expect I will have to sit in a launderette all day to keep warm. I will be a latchkey kid, whatever that is. And who will look after the dog? And what will I have to eat all day? I will be forced to eat crisps and sweets until my skin is ruined and my teeth fall out. I think my mother is being very selfish. She won't be any good in a job anyway. She isn't very bright and she drinks too much at Christmas." (21)
>
> Even though Adrian's mother does get a job, Adrian manages to survive, but by March he has another worry. School bully Barry Kent demands daily money from Adrian. On March 3, after Adrian pays off Barry, he

wonders how a fair God could let big kids like Barry go around being mean to smaller kids like Adrian. In trying to answer why such things happen, Adrian decides that,

"Perhaps their brains are easily worn out with all the extra work they have to do making bigger bones and stuff, or it could be that the big youths have got brain damage because of all the sport they play, or perhaps big youths just *like* menacing and fighting. When I go to university I may study the problem." (39)

Adrian's story is set in a suburban English town some twenty years ago when Englanders were excited about Charles and Diana's wedding, but at the same time were worried about the economic recession that causes Adrian's father to lose his job. Because of the British setting, you will have to work a little harder to figure out some of the terms as when Adrian takes on the project of assisting an OAP (Old Age Pensioner), when his class takes the M1 (Motorway 1) for a comically disastrous field trip to London, and when Adrian almost hopes that the RSPCA (Royal Society for Prevention of Cruelty to Animals) will come after his father for getting the dog drunk on Cherry Brandy. Adrian calls potato chips *crisps* and instead of just "going to the library," he has to "join the library," but in spite of such superficial differences as these, you will probably discover in your reading that American and British teenagers are more alike than they are different.

While *The Secret Diary of Adrian Mole Aged 13¾* hasn't disappeared, it is like so many of us thin people struggling to find a way out of our fat bodies. British author, Sue Townsend's first book was so successful that she has gone on to write five other books about Adrian Mole and so the first and the funniest sometimes gets lost in the crowd.

The version I read for this piece was packaged with two sequels through arrangements with the original publishers (Methuen London) under the title *Adrian Mole from Minor to Major: The Mole Diaries: The First Ten Years.* Besides the 1982 *Secret Diary*, it included the 1984 *Growing Pains of Adrian Mole* and the 1989 *Confessions of Adrian Mole*. These three books bring Adrian up to age 23¾. A better combination for American readers is the 1997 Avon pairing that includes only the first two titles, bringing Adrian up to age 18. Avon Flare has also re-released *The Secret Diary* by itself, while Econo-Clad offers library bound copies and Nicholas Barnes offers an audio cassette through *amazon.com*.

The Adrian Mole books were never intended as adolescent literature, which is a good-news/bad news story. The good news is that they aren't "written down" to kids so Townsend's creativity was not stymied by censorious editors asking whether particular words would ruin school sales and whether Adrian and his parents are proper role models. In fact, Adrian is a thoughtful and moral young man, though as one reviewer pointed out, not a *goody-good,* and what might have been considered "touchy" language in 1982 is pretty tame twenty years later. Gill Charles writing in *School Librarian*, when the book first came out, defended the language as providing a sense of authenticity and then illustrated how Townsend neatly side-stepped some problems as when Adrian writes, "I was sent out of the room then. It is a terrible thing to hear your own mother swearing" (383).

The bad news is that the books about the young Adrian Mole get confused with the ones about the "adult" Adrian Mole. When *The Secret Diary of Adrian Mole aged 13¾* first appeared, more than one reviewer predicted that it would develop the same kind of following as *The Catcher in the Rye*. I realize this is a trite prediction and that every year a half-dozen books are "honored" with such a prediction. Nevertheless, it makes me wonder where *Catcher* would be today if J. D. Salinger had written five sequels.

The later books go beyond the experiences and interests of teenagers. By book six, *Adrian Mole: The Cappuccino Years* (Soho, distributed by Farrar, 2000), Adrian is in his early 30's and is a divorced father of a three-year-old and a twelve-year-old. Besides the difference between the beginning and the end of what *Publisher's Weekly* described as Adrian's "lengthy and awkward passage from zit-ridden adolescence to angst-ridden manhood" (140), the later books aren't as much fun to read. This is because a necessary element of humor is surprise, and even though Sue Townsend is an amazingly clever and witty observer of daily life, after six books readers can't be so easily surprised.

Perhaps the best way to use *The Secret Diary of Adrian Mole Aged 13¾* in a class is to have five or six copies so that it can be part of a small group's reading, while the class as a whole focuses on the topic of literary humor. While one group reads and prepares an oral presentation on *The Secret Diary*, other groups could choose from *The True Confessions of Adrian Mole* and such humorous books as Gary Paulsen's *Harris and Me: A Summer Remembered* (Harcourt Brace, 1993), Ron Koertge's *The Arizona Kid* (Little, Brown, 1988), M. E. Kerr's *If I Love You, Am I*

Trapped Forever? (HarperCollins, 1973), Robert Kaplow's *Alex Icicle: A Romance in Ten Torrid Chapters* (Houghton, Mifflin, 1984), Daniel Pinkwater's *The Snarkout Boys and the Avocado of Death* (Lothrop, 1982), and Francesca Lia Block's *Weetzie Bat* (HarperCollins, 1989).

When *The Secret Diary* was first published, reviewers used such descriptors as "the side-splitting odyssey of Adrian Mole" (*Publishers Weekly*), a "very funny . . . wide slice of reality, good and bad . . . which should prove appealing to even the most reluctant reader" (*School Librarian*), and "extremely funny, insightful, self-pitying, egotistical, yet appealing" (*School Library Journal*). Nevertheless, when presenting the book to students, you will want to walk a fine line between enticing readers with its humor and setting them up for disappointment.

Literary humor is not the same as humor presented by stand-up comedians, which means that students need to be gently led to appreciate some of the qualities that are connected with the slower, more subtle humor found in novels. One of the chief differences is the fuller development of characterization. The fact that readers know so much about Adrian and his parents, as well as about his heart's desire (appropriately named Pandora) and about his elderly friend Bert Baxter, allows them to enjoy what comedians now refer to as "alternative comedy." Rather than being a line-up of jokes that one might find on the Internet or in a script passed from one comedian to another, alternative comedy is unique to a particular performer and situation. This idea is what literary humor is all about, and the best of it does what Malcolm Muggeridge, an intellectual idol that Adrian writes to but does not get an answer from, said he was always looking for when he edited *Punch* magazine. He wanted humor that would make people laugh for ten seconds and think for ten minutes.

Critics are making some obvious comparisons between Adrian Mole's humor and that of a fourteen-year-old girl in a more recent British import: Louise Rennison's *Angus, Thongs and Full-Frontal Snogging: Confessions of Georgia Nicolson* (HarperCollins, 2000). The books are similar in that the protagonists are the same age and they dwell incessantly on the condition of their skin and the sexual urges inspired by their newly developed hormones. Also both books are written in the format of short diary entries, and they are so full of British slang that readers need a glossary. While the new book is likely to attract more readers because of its sexy cover, I'm old-fashioned enough to prefer the more subtle Adrian Mole story. Adrian's story seems more honest because readers get to know him as a fully developed individual whose sexual questions and fantasies are only a relatively small part of his story.

BIBLIOGRAPHY

Black, Nancy E. Review of *The Secret Diary of Adrian Mole Aged 13¾*. *School Library Journal* 31, no. 1 (September, 1984): 134.

Dingley, Robert. "Sue Townsend: Overview." 650-71 in *Twentieth-Century Young Adult Writers,* 1st ed., edited by Laura Standley Berger. Detroit, Michigan: St. James Press, 1994.

Gale Group Contempory Authors Online. Susan Elaine Townsend, 1946, Entry Updated June 5, 2001.

Charles, Gill. Review of *The Secret Diary of Adrian Mole Aged 13¾*. *School Librarian* 31, no. 4 (December, 1983): 383.

Lahr, John. "A Female Trickster." *New Society* 63, no. 1062 (March 24, 1983): 474-75.

Review of *The Secret Diary of Adrian Mole Aged 13¾*. *Publishers Weekly* 225, no. 8 (February 24, 1984): 140.

Rennison, Louise. *Angus, Thongs and Full-Frontal Snogging: Confessions of Georgia Nicolson.*
New York: HarperCollins, 2000.

Seaman, Donna. *Review of Adrian Mole: The Cappuccino Years*. *Booklist* 96, no. 21 (July, 2000): 1977.

Townsend, Sue. *Adrian Mole From Minor to Major The Mole Diaries: The First Ten Years.* London: Mandarin Paperbacks, 1991.

Alleen Pace Nilsen is co-author with Ken Donelson of *Literature for Today's Young Adults*, a pioneering textbook for teachers and librarians, now in its sixth edition from Longman. She teaches in the English department at Arizona State University and has written over fifty published articles and reviews about teenagers and the books they read.

Chapter Eleven

Belonging to a Place: *Home Before Dark* by Sue Ellen Bridgers

Connie S. Zitlow

In a beautifully written story first published in 1976 but just as powerful today, Stella Willis' greatest adventure is riding in an Impala Chevrolet with a boy on each side.[1] What gives this seemingly small event such significance in the novel *Home Before Dark*? Readers feel an intangible swelling of emotion with Stella; they understand her excitement, the thrill she feels when she takes this ride, because it is so different from the ride she is taking when her story begins. Stella and her mom, dad, brothers William and Earl, and baby sister Lissy arrive at her father's family tobacco farm in eastern North Carolina, all crowded in a hot and battered old station wagon. Fourteen-year-old Stella is tired of living out of the car as her family has moved from one place to another to pick whatever crops are ready for harvest. Everything the family owns is in the car, and all they have is each other. But Stella is headed home, and she declares, "I'm never leaving."[2]

Stella is headstrong and proud, "thin and fair, with the dingy, fading pallor of intermittent sunburns to her skin. She looked like a discarded doll, with dry fibre hair, that had been endowed with human eyelids which were puffy and red from hours of restless sleep in the car" (*Home*, 2). She is determined to have roots and to be part of the life her father, James Earl Willis, abandoned sixteen years before. Stella thinks the empty tenant house at the end of a lane on Uncle Newton's farm is wonderful. As her family moves in, she finds the place to which she belongs:

> She had been born a squalling knot of tight, unexplainable longings that screamed "I will be" to a world that seemed to ignore her, that gave her no safety but the battered shell of an automobile and an armrest on which

to pound her silent anger. Now she had a place to store the secret Stella and draw her longings out slowly, carefully, one by one, and keep them safe. She would never desert this place, never let it slip away as her daddy had. They could all vanish, and she would stay, because already what counted for her was here, inside walls that didn't move in the dark or carry her somewhere as strange and unwelcoming as the last place she'd been. (*Home*, 15)

Everything Stella wanted, her mother Mae rejected. Powerless, disconnected Mae had never had time for companionship or a sense of self, never had a homeplace, and she despises the house.[3] Mae cannot adjust to a stationary life and is afraid of losing the closeness of the life her family shared when they were all together in a dusty white station wagon. She wanted to go "away from a life that would require something of her" (*Home*, 42). When Mae is killed by lightning, Stella wonders, "Do you think she wanted it to happen? She didn't like it here, you know" (*Home*, 77).

The first real friend Stella has ever had is Toby, whose family lives and works on the Willis farm. Toby is bright and charmed by Stella, who talks him into helping her paint the tenant house. "Loving Stella was the hardest thing he had ever done" (*Home*, 67), but Toby seems to know he is only a farmhand. Toby is the one who comforts Stella when Mae dies, but it is rich, well-dressed, awkward Rodney Biggers who becomes Stella's first boyfriend and with whom she shares her first kiss. Taking her thrilling ride in Rodney's car, sandwiched between him and Toby, Stella experiences a new feeling, one of freedom, as the wind blows through her hair, and she has what for her is the greatest adventure.

Ironically it is Mae's death that is the impetus for the family's liberation from poverty when later Stella's father, James Earl, marries an old school friend, the lonely Maggie Grover, who owns a store, a big house, and longs for a husband and children. For a time, Stella refuses to leave the land, the place where she belongs, and move to town with the rest of her family:

> She wouldn't leave this little house for Maggie Grover's leaden world. She wouldn't set her feet off this land or desert the blood-stained mattress of a grandmother she'd never known. She wouldn't. . . . For she knew, as surely as her mother had known the road was home, that this shotgun frame was where her life was. She wouldn't leave it. (*Home*, 122)

But Stella finally does realize that the little house on the farm is only one part of her life. She can go back to it, but she realizes she must go *from* there, too. She learns that roots and love are more than a house, and what she feels about her homeplace will go with her. Readers see that Stella's move is more than a physical one. She moves from a focus on tragedy and loss to one of personal growth.

With the publication of *Home Before Dark*, her first book, Sue Ellen Bridgers celebrated her own homeplace in the tobacco country of eastern North Carolina. Because she was homesick as she wrote the story, its setting was particularly important to her, and she considered the land a character in the story.[4] In her novels, all set in the rural South, Bridgers has written about life in families. The difference between Stella and her mother and the loving, caring feelings between Stella and her father, who gives her time and space after Mae's death, are examples of Bridgers's exploration of the various relationships within families. Members of her own extended family are an important part of her life. The compassion, resilience, and courage of the women in her life, particularly her mother and grandmother, made a deep impression on her. In her stories she studies women and the connections to the ones they love. With family life as the core of her writing, she celebrates the opportunities and achievements of women and a wide circle of family and close friends, men and women, who add security, acceptance, and love to one's life.[5] Similarly Stella is drawn to her aunt and uncle who have remained on the family farm and from whom she learns about her grandmother and her roots.

The author of seven award-winning novels for adults and young adults, numerous short stories, screenplays, and beautifully written, inspiring articles, Bridgers is a literary artist who cares deeply about her characters. They become a real person to her, beginning with a visual impression, a physical presence that triggers her interest and imagination.[6] She thinks about them in human terms and explores the person inside events, the internal conflicts they feel as they consider what choices they have in life. She has said that because her characters' external lives are frequently limited to ordinary experiences that hardly seem book-worthy, if anything gives them significance, it is the internal decisions they must make, the choices and accompanying responsibilities that affect their emotional well-being ("Life," 3).

For Bridgers the essentials of making a book are time, place, the human element of character, and her commitment "to create the work she has envisioned, in particular rather than general terms" ("Stories Two," 55). There are many examples of vivid imagery in *Home Before Dark* that place readers in the midst of the setting where they see, feel, and hear what the characters experience: "At night, when the house was hushed with breathing and the feathering of moth wings against the screens, James Earl lay awake" (*Home*, 89). When Stella hears Maggie singing to Lissy, "she knew she was hearing the sound of love. Never had she heard it so clearly before, not in textbook poems or in love scenes on flickering movie screens, not even in her daddy's voice when it came to her across the muffled sound of babies breathing in the night. It was music—richly, harmoniously, undeniable true" (*Home, 145–46*). It is this same particularity that transports Bridgers's stories beyond one location.

As a person and as an author, Bridgers radiates warmth and a deep concern for young people everywhere, whose view of the universal human experience is broadened as they hear the lyric Southern voice in her stories. Apparent in all of Bridgers's work is her intellect, her memory and vivid imagination, and her desire to show readers that they have choices, regardless of others' expectations. Although they become immersed in the lives of her very human characters in a certain time and place, readers realize the concerns and experiences of the young people in her stories are not restricted to any one setting. Not all teens have had experiences like Stella's: living the life of a migrant family, helping her mother give birth and later seeing her die, discovering the mattress where her cancer-ridden grandmother committed suicide. But young people understand what it means to want to belong somewhere, to need family and friends, to ask who they are or what will happen to them. They certainly understand Toby's developing sexuality and emphasize with Stella's feelings of joy, sadness, her confusion as she is caught between caring about two boys, and her determination to change her life.

In addition to her importance as a writer for young adults, Bridgers, the storyteller, also belongs with other contemporary Southern writers who are noted for their writing skill.[7] Her artistry for telling universal stories in a distinctive and lyrical Southern voice has won her high critical acclaim and numerous awards. In 1985 the Assembly on Literature for Adolescents of the National Council of Teachers of English honored Bridgers for her outstanding contributions to young adult literature. Although she does not begin her stories writing for a certain audience, she feels a great responsibility to give young people her best: "Books that reflect their concerns, that give them characters they can learn from or identify with, language both clear and inventive that they can emulate" ("Notes," 45). She believes that "young adult books not only help young people grow emotionally but also contribute enormously to their becoming better readers and writers."[8] But for a book to contribute to readers' growth, it must have a reader—and it must be in print and available—or it has no life.

Unfortunately, at times Bridgers's works, including *Home Before Dark*, have been out of print or difficult to obtain. Readers must not lose the chance to hear the music of her words, see the settings and vivid images she portrays, feel the deep emotions of her characters, become immersed in complex family connections, and ponder the choices, responsibilities, burdens, friendships, and identity issues of her characters. Young readers understand more about what life is for others and what it can be for them when they find parts of themselves in her stories and when they think about the themes that transcend time and place.

NOTES

1. Sue Ellen Bridgers, "Writing for My Life," *The ALAN Review* 23, no. 1 (Fall 1995): 4; hereafter cited in text as "Life."

2. Sue Ellen Bridgers, *Home Before Dark* (New York: Bantam Books, 1976), 15; hereafter cited in text as *Home*.

3. Sue Ellen Bridgers, "Stories My Grandmother Told Me: Part One," *The ALAN Review* 13, no. 1 (Fall 1985): 47.

4. Connie S. Zitlow and Tobie R. Sanders, "Conversations with Robert Cormier and Sue Ellen Bridgers: Their Life and Work as Writers," *Ohio Journal of the English Language Arts* 39, no. 2 (Winter/Spring 1999): 34-48.

5. Sue Ellen Bridgers, "Stories My Grandmother Told Me: Part Two," *The ALAN Review* 13, no. 2 (Winter 1986): 55; hereafter cited in text as "Stories Two."

6. Sue Ellen Bridgers, "Notes from a Guerilla," *English Journal* 88, no. 6 (July 1999): 42; hereafter cited in text as "Notes."

7. Ted Hipple, *Presenting Sue Ellen Bridgers* (Boston: Twayne Publishers, 1990), 96-100.

8. Sue Ellen Bridgers, "Creating a Bond Between Writer and Reader," in *Reading Their World,* ed. Virginia Monseau and Gary Salvner (Portsmouth, NH: Boynton/Cook, 1992), 70.

BIBLIOGRAPHY

Bridgers, Sue Ellen. *Home Before Dark*. New York: Bantam, 1976. (Now available from Banks Channel Books)
———. "Stories My Grandmother Told Me: Part One." *The ALAN Review* 13, no. 1 (Fall 1985): 44-48.
———. "Stories My Grandmother Told Me: Part Two." *The ALAN Review* 13, no. 2 (Winter 1986): 53-55.
———. "Creating a Bond Between Writer and Reader." 65-70 in *Reading Their World: The Young Adult Novel in the Classroom*, ed. Virginia R. Monseau and Gary M. Salvner. Portsmouth, NH: Boynton/Cook Publishers, 1992.
———. "Writing for My Life." *The ALAN Review* 23, no. 1 (Fall 1995): 2-7.
———. "Notes from a Guerrilla." *English Journal* 88, no. 6 (July 1999): 41-47.
Hipple, Ted. *Presenting Sue Ellen Bridgers*. Boston: Twayne Publishers, 1990.
Zitlow, Connie S. and Tobie R. Sanders. "Conversations with Robert Cormier and Sue Ellen Bridgers: Their Life and Work as Writers." *The Ohio Journal of the English Language Arts* 39, no. 2 (Winter/Spring 1999): 34-50.

Connie S. Zitlow is a professor at Ohio Wesleyan University where she teaches courses in young adult literature, content area reading, and teaching methods, and directs the secondary education program. Her publications about young adult literature have appeared in numerous books and journals, and she served as the 2000 president of ALAN. She currently edits the "Professional Links" column for *English Journal*.

Chapter Twelve

The Law and Magic: Searching for Incantations in Sol Stein's *The Magician*

Margaret J. Ford and Susan L. Stevens

With the resounding echo of a judge's gavel rather than a mystical incantation, *The Magician* disappeared from publication and was lost, at a critical time in its publication history, to young adult audiences. In a Chapter Eleven bankruptcy battle whose questionable justice ironically mirrored the theme of *The Magician*, author Sol Stein was legally prohibited from reprinting or selling copies of his disturbing novel. Large pre-paid book orders from school wholesalers around the country were turned away. A banned book whose power is reminiscent of *The Chocolate War, After the First Death*, or *Ironman* was effectively silenced until Stein regained publishing rights after a three-year hiatus. Twenty years after it first appeared, it was reprinted as an Author's Guild Backinprint.com edition of *iUniverse.com*.

Ed Japhet, the sixteen-year-old protagonist, is a teen magician whose performance at his high school prom exacerbates an already tenuous relationship between rivals and results in an attack on him, his girlfriend, and his father as they leave the dance. Ed's poise, skill, and refusal to share the mystery of his magic are the final affronts to Stanley Urek, leader of a school gang whose members have extorted protection money from every other member of the school except Ed. Urek attacks Ed's girlfriend, bashes in his father's windshield, and nearly chokes Ed to death with a tire chain before he and the rest of the gang flee into the night. Urek later invades Ed's intensive care hospital room and severs what he believes is Ed's air hose in a further attempt to kill him. Urek's father Paul wisely retains the town's brightest and best attorney, George Thomassy, to defend his son. The remainder of the novel chronicles the legal slight-of-hand Thomassy, a character in several other books by

Stein, employs to gain his client's acquittal at the expense of justice. In effect, it becomes the story of two magicians who ironically battle to define the law—as majesty or trickery—in the working class community of Ossining, New York, home of one the nation's best-known prisons—Sing Sing.

Originally published in 1971 by Delacorte Press, *The Magician* was a selection of the Book-of-the-Month Club. It enjoyed healthy sales and was a popular classroom choice, eventually surpassing the half-million mark.[1] The novel was generally well received by reviewers both here and abroad and was recommended for inclusion in young adult collections by *Library Journal*.[2] Critics, perhaps reflecting the turmoil and mistrust of the seventies, applauded Stein's thematic concept. *Booklist* congratulated *The Magician* for "effectively underscoring the escalation of violence in the U. S. and the irrelevance of justice to the judicial system."[3] The novel "emphasizes the increasing indifference of U. S. citizens and legal and educational institutions toward helpless victims of violence."[4] Certainly, in the wake of militia-style violence and school tragedies, these same observations might hold true today.

Other critics, while acknowledging the thematic strength of the novel, feel some of the situations improbable[5] and find some of the characters undeveloped.[6] Reviewer Aaron L. Fessler observes that "so intent is he on the irony of the case that he permits one or two improbabilities to creep into the otherwise fine-structured plot, but they do not dull the point he is making."[7] Certainly, the scene during which Stanley Urek is revealed as Ed Japhet's attacker by the school principal in the middle of a school assembly is improbable, even considering school policy of the seventies. Many of the reviewers who took exception to Stein's lack of character development were referring to the minor characters he introduces and then seems to drop. Rather than detracting from the strength of the novel, this appeared to ring true of student life both then and now. There would certainly be students like Jerry Samuelson, an ambitious student stringer for the *New York Times*, who sees Urek's attack as an opportunity for advancement. There would be adults like Dr. Gunther Koch following the events at a distance and perhaps interjecting his presence in the name of personal research. In fact, stylistically, the insertion of these characters and their first-person narrative observations provides some interesting shifts in point of view.

The novel remained a popular classroom choice throughout its initial sixteen-year publishing history despite a high-profile ban in Wisconsin, which Stein and Dell Publishing Company, the publisher of the paperback edition, handled in a very creative way. To gain support for the book, they offered a free copy to every household in Montello, Wisconsin, where the book had been banned. Ultimately, the school board voted to permit the use of the book although parental permission was required.[8] The teacher whose use of the book was called into question had used the book in conjunction with a reading of *To Kill a Mockingbird* as "examples of different outlooks on American justice that would 'help a student to become a critical reader.' The novels, she said, would also alert students to the existence of 'the struggle to restrain violence in society and in ourselves.'"[9] Certainly, these are concerns that are still at issue in schools today. Stanley Urek's portrayal as a bully who extorts money from students with the benign consent of the school administration is an even hotter issue today given the recent cases of school violence.

All the key points that garnered critical comment are the very issues that recommend the continued use of *The Magician* in its reprinted version. The novel, which illustrates the divide among Americans regarding class, education, and religion, deliberately and painfully exposes the injustice of legal loopholes for victims too naïve or too exhausted by the failure of the judicial system to employ similar tricks. George Thomassy systematically finds weaknesses in the potential witnesses against Urek and exploits those flaws to discourage them from testifying or to discredit their testimony. Thomassy visits Alice Ginsler, a nurse's aide who can place Urek at the scene of a second attack on Ed Japhet, to suggest that her communal lifestyle might be revealed and affect her credibility as a witness if she were questioned on the stand. She decides not to testify.

Thomassy pays an investigator to find out why Terrence Japhet, Ed's father, was denied a State Department job. He cross-examines him and reveals he was not considered because he had lied on his employment application, exaggerating his foreign travel experience. Although this incident had nothing to do with his credibility as an eyewitness to his son's brutal attack, Thomassy once again manipulates the situation to his client's advantage. Thomassy's skill, rather than the truth of the situation, leads to Urek's acquittal. At the end of the novel, when Ed kills Urek in self-defense during a third attack, Terrence Japhet is no longer naïve and idealistic—he calls Thomassy to defend his son. When justice fails, trust in trickery.

In the numerous first-person narratives that are subtitled at various points in the text, characters have an opportunity to share their thoughts and reflections. What is striking about all of them is not a sense of apathy but a sense of resignation to oppressive forces over which they have no control. Mr. Chadwick, the school principal, comments on Urek's extortion racket:

> Yes, I know about the locker-room business, and I don't know how to stop it. If I issued another edict, it would have the same effect as the first: nothing. We never see them taking money from the students . . . there's been no fatality at the school as yet.[10]

Other such first-person narratives share personal failures, weaknesses, or ambitions. Many, like Mr. Chadwick's piece, also mirror the injustices that can be found in the larger community. If adults can't control what goes on in the schools, how can they rectify mob violence, racial prejudice, and the class struggles that can be found in communities throughout the country?

Stein often juxtaposes asides that might be construed as inflammatory as he plays with social stereotypes. Paul Urek, Stanley's father, is portrayed as a Redneck. Ed's friend Gil who visits him in the hospital before he returns to his army base observes that

> the army is full of guys like that, Rednecks, from every part of the country. Beer, bowling, hunting, car Simonizing. You should hear them talk about women, even their wives. Filling the old lady's hole, is the way they think of it. These guys don't even go to the movies, except drive-ins, and that's not for the movies. Biggest thing they miss in the army is TV. Booze and poker, that's it.[11]

Stein later follows up on this stereotype when Paul Urek recruits some of his buddies from the bowling alley to trash the teens' rec hall as a reprisal for a letter to the editor that decries the fear under which law-abiding students must attend school.

In addition to the issues that still seem to pervade classrooms across the country, the novel has great impact as a story of the seventies. It could effectively be paired with other novels, films, and nonfiction accounts of the decade and the Vietnam War. As Terrence Japhet surveys the posters decorating the walls of his son's room, he sees

> Hendrix, dead. Joplin, dead. Zappa sitting on a toilet. The idiot boy from *Mad* magazine, wearing an Uncle Sam uniform and saying, 'Who Needs YOU?' And on the facing wall, Dennis Hopper and Peter Fonda on their

strangely shaped cycles smiling easily as they ride toward a gratuitous death.[11]

Who graces the walls of young adults across the country today?

Of course, the issues that caused the book to be banned in Wisconsin are still controversies today. There is profanity, although not gratuitous. There are explicit sexual references that would make this book a choice for mature students. However, the power of the theme, style, and characterization make *The Magician* an important "lost" novel to consider returning to the classroom now that it has been rescued from the backlist that tangled it in Stein's Chapter Eleven bankruptcy case. The persona of Ed Japhet as magician and his reflection on that role sums up the potential and the power of the novel:

> Ed had hated the magicians he had seen at school and in shows. Having lost their sense of surprise, their hands darted gracelessly, their chatter became mechanical. A magician, Ed felt, needed to believe anew that each trick really worked, just as the audience did. Like life, in magic there was always the unpredictable.[12]

The Magician is certainly proof of that.

NOTES

1. Sol Stein, "The Return of 'The Magician,'" *The New Leader,* 10 (24 December 1990): 19-20.
2. Alberta Hankenson, "The Magician," Review, *Library Journal* 96, (15 October 1971): 3489.
3. "The Magician; a novel" *Booklist* 68 (15 October1971): 191.
4. "The Magician; a novel" *Booklist* 68 (1 October1971): 132.
5. Aaron L. Fessler, "The Magician," Review, *Library Journal* 97 (15 February 1972): 700
6. Webster Schott, "Man in the Role of Destroyer: The Magician." *New York Times Book Review* (26 September 1971): 53.
7. Fessler, "The Magician."
8. "Sol Stein and Dell Offer Free Copies of Novel to Wisconsin Families snarled in Book Banning," *Publisher's Weekly* 219 (3 April 1983): 14.
9. "Sol Stein and Dell Offer Free Copies..." *Publishers Weekly*
10. Sol Stein, *The Magician* (Lincoln, NE: *iUniverse.com*, Inc., 2000), 21.
11. Stein, 182.
12. Stein, 11.

Susan Stevens directs the Jennings Urban Fellows project, a collaborative project between Kent State University and the Youngstown City Schools, focusing on improving instruction for urban middle school students. She has taught young adult literature in a variety of settings from middle school through university, is the past president of the Western Reserve of Ohio Teachers of English, and was recognized by the Ohio Council of Teachers of English Language Arts (OCTELA) as Outstanding High School English Teacher in 1995.

Margaret Ford is the District Library/Media Specialist for Campbell City Schools, Campbell, Ohio, where she taught English/language arts for twenty-three years. She is an adjunct faculty member at Youngstown State University where she teaches entry-level composition courses. She is a past president of OCTELA, a recipient of OCTELA's Outstanding English Language Arts Educator Educator award, and regularly reviews texts for *The ALAN Review*.

Chapter Thirteen

Sharon Bell Mathis's *Listen for the Fig Tree:* A Timeless YA Novel

Pamela Sissi Carroll

In 1980, I was a new teacher, working with a group of high school juniors who in today's parlance would be labeled "at risk" students. That was the year that I first taught a novel by Sharon Bell Mathis, *Teacup Full of Roses*. In a rural Alabama high school, the predominantly African American male population of my class liked Mathis's book, not because they were familiar with the setting (an inner-city ghetto), not because they enjoyed reading fiction (or anything at all), but because they saw themselves in Mathis's three protagonists—black brothers who were trying to make a life for themselves, despite harsh surroundings and daily threats to their survival. For those students, Mathis's novel was real. After several days of listening to me read aloud to the absorbed class, Lindsey, who had neither volunteered nor spoken for at least twelve weeks, politely interrupted, asking, "Can I take a turn reading out loud, now?" The novel, its author, Lindsey, and his classmates, had connected. I was tempted to contact Mathis, who was a special education teacher in Washington, D.C. and Writer-in-Residence at Howard University at the time, to share the readers' enthusiastic responses with her.

The next year, at a different high school, I taught Mathis's *Listen for the Fig Tree*. Ninth-graders who were talented, enthusiastic readers, along with their reluctant reader classmates, were captivated by the themes and topics that Mathis addresses in this novel. Few of the students had ever before used a literary work as a springboard for discussion of single-parent families, the impact of murder on survivors, racial discrimination from two angles, positive characteristics of a caring gay man, how friendship works, or how they might react if they lost their sight. Again, students connected with a book by Mathis. *Listen for the Fig Tree* is a powerful novel; it is time that we re-examine it and then introduce it to a new generation of adolescent readers.

Marvina "Muffin" Johnson is an African American girl living in a low-income Brooklyn neighborhood. Born with poor vision, Muffin loses her sight completely as she enters adolescence. Her father, a cab driver, is murdered; her mother, Leola, believes that his death was never investigated because he was black. Leola falls into a deep depression, especially on the Christmas Eve anniversary of the murder. She goes on destructive drinking binges and leaves her strong yet vulnerable daughter to take on the role of the adult in the family. Mr. Dale, a flamboyant neighbor who appears to be gay, is Muffin's most trusted friend. He insists that she walk proudly, with respect for herself and her heritage; he helps Muffin nurse her drunken mother out of an alcohol-induced stupor; he promises to buy her a guide dog when she turns eighteen. And Mr. Dale uses his talent and enthusiasm for creating splendid clothing from scraps to ensure that Muffin will attend a Christmas/Kwanza festival in African regalia.

Listen for the Fig Tree deserves renewed attention for three primary reasons: its themes and topics transcend temporal boundaries and challenge the thinking of teens even today; its literary quality is high; and its focus on a teen who has vision impairment encourages readers to contemplate life through a different set of lenses. Further, today's adolescent reader will find interesting references to fashions of the 1970s in Mathis's book. While details about clothing and hairstyle and even slang words date *Listen for the Fig Tree*, they provide an interesting point of departure for study of changes in a community's culture, or a starting point for an interdisciplinary focus on the ways that fashion, even in slang, have changed over the past several decades.

In *Listen for the Fig Tree*, as in Virginia Euwer Wolff's *Make Lemonade*, Norma Fox Mazer's *When She Was Good*, and Jacqueline Woodson's Coretta Scott King Award winning *I Hadn't Meant to Tell You This*, readers meet a young girl who is forced by life's circumstances to accept adult responsibilities. Muffin's sense of humor and of hope, like LaVaughn's in *Make Lemonade*, fluctuates with an awareness of ugly inevitabilities. Both characters must push schooling from the forefront of their concerns in order to help care for others. Like Em in *When She Was Good*, Muffin must contend with the demands of a family member who is unpredictable and often self-destructive. Like Marie in *I Hadn't*

Meant to Tell You This, Muffin is an African American young adolescent with a hurtful family secret. In each of these books, a young girl's coming of age is accelerated by her life's circumstances. Mathis's realistic treatment of this theme is authentic and timeless.

As they read *Listen for the Fig Tree,* some contemporary readers will choose to examine the life and perspective of an African American teen who is living in inner-city poverty. Readers who meet Greg Harris in Walter Dean Myers's explosive *SLAM!* might choose to compare and contrast Greg's world with Muffin's. Other readers might focus on generational relationships between women in an African American family. This relationship, as portrayed by Mathis, resonates with the relationship among three generations of African American women in Angela Johnson's lyrical *Toning the Sweep.*

Mathis's novel is also a work of literary art that compares favorably with, for example, Mildred D. Taylor's YA fiction. In *Listen for the Fig Tree,* we read beautifully crafted passages in which metaphoric language emerges, similar to the language we find in Taylor's books about Cassie Logan, beginning with the Newbery Medal winning *Roll of Thunder, Hear My Cry,* which was followed by *Let the Circle Be Unbroken,* and *The Road to Memphis.* The affectionate terms that Mr. Dale uses for Muffin, such as "Sweet Black Muffin Child. Plum of my life," (22) and "Muffin, My Lifesong," (94) provide brief glimpses of Mathis's use of figurative language. The fact that both authors have focused on African American females is serendipitous, but it does provide another point of comparison.

A third compelling reason to revisit *Listen for the Fig Tree* is that in this novel Mathis leads readers to contemplate how an adolescent—one who is vision-impaired—navigates in a sight-oriented world. Mathis's attention to this issue has been raised recently in YA books as varied as Jeanette Ingold's *The Window,* and Edward Bloor's *Tangerine.* Muffin does not let blindness define her; instead, she uses routine and her other senses to help her complete daily activities. When she cooks a Christmas dinner, for example, she relies effectively on a carefully constructed plan, on her hearing:

> Muffin opened a cupboard and took out the timers she wanted. . . . And minutes later, Muffin was dumping two packages of special stew spices into an earthen bowl half-filled with beef chunks. Then she put flour and more spices into a paper lunch bag and put in the pieces of meat and

shook the bag up and down. Then she plopped each floured cube into a huge iron pot of sizzling fat. When the meat was crusty-edged, tested by Muffin's forking each piece and touching her finger to it quickly, she poured water in the pot and put the heavy lid on and turned the fire low. (*Listen for the Fig Tree,* 115)

Because of her blindness, adolescent readers might expect Muffin to give in to the urge to rely too heavily on her mother or another adult; however, Muffin expects no less of herself than she expects of others. For example, when her mother is sick after a night of drinking, Muffin takes charge in a matter-of-fact manner:

She would have to wash all of the floors except the kitchen—and maybe even the kitchen. . . . Her mother had gotten sick there too, on much of the sink. . . . The second thing she had to do was clean her mother up. But Muffin washed her own face first and tried to feel better. Vomit was vomit. It wasn't blood. (92)

During the story, Muffin begins to realize an essential truth: she cannot take responsibility for her mother's unwise and self-destructive actions and attitudes. Like other adolescents, she has to reconcile the tug between dependence on her mother, and independence. Muffin has a best girlfriend, a boyfriend, and adults whom she trusts. Like most adolescents, she also must deal with some significant problems. Mathis's three-dimensional characterization allows readers to see that being blind does not prevent an adolescent from being attracted—or attractive—to sighted teens and adults and their world, to being a part of their world.[1]

With themes and topics that are as potent today as when the novel was first published in 1974, with literary quality that rewards classroom attention, and with its insights about living without sight, Sharon Bell Mathis's *Listen for the Fig Tree* deserves a place on the bookshelves of today's adolescent readers and in middle and high school classrooms.

Sharon Bell Mathis often credits her mother, a poet, with her love of words, and a perch on the fire escape, overlooking the Bedford Stuyesant neighborhood where she grew up, as the place where she discovered reading. Now retired, the former teacher and librarian is a founding member of the children's literature division of the Washington, D.C. Black Writers' Workshop. Recently, her recognition has emerged from the success of her children's books. She was awarded the Coretta Scott King Award for the biography *Ray Charles* (Crowell, 1973). A popular recent children's book of hers is *Running Girl: The Diary of Ebonee Rose* (Browndeer Harcourt, 1997).

NOTE

1. For more information on characters with vision impairment as they are portrayed in YA books, please see Pamela S. Carroll and L. Penny Rosenblum, "Through Their Eyes: Are Characters with Visual Impairment Portrayed Realistically in Young Adult Literature?" in *Journal of Adolescent and Adult Literacy*, 42 (7), April, 2000, 620-30.

BIBLIOGRAPHY

Johnson, Angela. *Toning the Sweep*. New York: Scholastic, 1993.
Mathis, Sharon Bell. *Listen For the Fig Tree*. New York: Viking, 1974. (reissued by Puffin Books in 1990.)
———. *Teacup Full of Roses*. New York: Viking, 1972.
Mazer, Norma Fox. *When She Was Good*. New York: Scholastic, 1997.
Myers, Walter Dean. *SLAM!* New York: Scholastic, 1996.
Taylor, Mildred D. *Roll of Thunder, Hear My Cry*. New York: Dial, 1976.
———. *Let the Circle Be Unbroken*. New York: Dial, 1981.
———. *The Road to Memphis*. New York: Dial, 1990.
Wolff, Virginia Euwer. *Make Lemonade*. New York: Scholastic, 1993.
Woodson, Jacqueline. *I Hadn't Meant to Tell You This*. New York: Bantam Doubleday Dell, 1994.

A former teacher of middle and high school English/language arts, **Pamela Sissi Carroll** is currently professor and coordinator of English education at Florida State University, where she teaches courses that focus on bringing young adult and canonical literature into classrooms in lively and meaningful ways. She is the editor of *The ALAN Review*, and author of *Caroline Cooney: Faith and Fiction* (Scarecrow, 2001), and other works on young adult books.

Chapter Fourteen

Humanity and Its Discontents in *The Keeper of the Isis Light* by Monica Hughes

Leila Christenbury

The Keeper of the Isis Light, published over twenty years ago, is the first of Canadian writer Monica Hughes's Isis trilogy (*The Guardian of Isis*, the Phoenix Award-winning *The Isis Pedlar*, and *Isis Light*). While still in print—and even at one point translated into German and Japanese— this science fiction classic is neither widely used nor widely quoted, and it is hoped that pieces such as this one will bring the book back to its rightful place as one of the gems of young adult literature.

There are a number of qualities that make *The Keeper of the Isis Light* so compelling. The major characters are brilliantly sketched; the use of image and description is superior; the plot is suspenseful and even unpredictable; the conclusion is unexpected; and the themes are central to young readers' concerns. In essence, *The Keeper of the Isis Light* looks at questions of humanity, notably the issues of being human, of losing innocence, and of valuing outside appearance. Reading the book can lead to rich discussions about all these topics, and, further, students can consider the extent to which the novel's conclusion is convincing and realistic.

The Keeper of the Isis Light has gained critical acclaim and was placed on the Best Book List for Young Adults by the American Library Association in 1981 and on the Honor List by the International Board on Books for Young People in 1982. Despite Hughes's possible stumble at the novel's end (which I explore further in subsequent pages), I rank *The Keeper of the Isis Light* among my top ten young adult novels.

As the book opens, Olwen Pendennis, sixteen, is getting ready to celebrate her birthday. We learn that she lives in a perfect, albeit isolated and uninhabited world, the beautiful and also occasionally hostile planet Isis, a planet with multiple moons, an intense, ultraviolet light, a twenty-hour day, blue green sky, orange mountains, silvery gray grass, sharp rocks and thorns, and a very thin atmosphere.

Hughes paints an idyllic but not cloying life. On Isis, attended by her faithful companion, Guardian, and her beloved dog, Hobbit, Olwen resides in a mansion crafted of polished rock and filled with clothes, furniture, music, and food designed by Guardian for her amusement and education. An orphan of human parents, the thoughtful but somewhat indulged Olwen is the center of Guardian's life: he promised her dying parents to care for her, and he spends his time attending to her needs. Guardian is dispassionate and steady, an ideal adult caretaker whose emotional stability and consistent logic are excellent foils for Olwen's occasional bursts of youthful impatience.

For her part, while Olwen vaguely remembers her dead parents—geological researchers who perished in one of Isis's occasional, violent planetary storms—she is content, and the description of the ways in which Guardian keeps her so is detailed and rich, from the musical dress he makes for her birthday celebration to the jewelry he carves for her adornment.

But Olwen and Guardian also have employment. Since she was a child, Olwen has been the Keeper of the Isis Light, the person who transmits daily information about her planet's weather, events, and even a personal report to the outside world. The work is steady but not onerous and is geared to the possible arrival of colonizers, traveling from overcrowded Earth to set up a settlement on the somewhat habitable Isis. Guardian, foreshadowing the book's major conflict, reminds Olwen about this eventuality. Shortly after her birthday, the earthly colonizers do indeed land on Isis and, with them, bring disruption and the eventual destruction of Olwen and Guardian's solitary Eden.

While Olwen knows it is her duty to work with the colonizers, like any young person fearing change, she is sullen and resentful regarding their arrival. Nevertheless, she attempts to help them. In particular, the seventeen-year-old Mark intrigues her, and they enter into a traditional teenage romance very quickly. Mark is the first real intrusion into Olwen's serene universe, and she experiences all the worries, about what she says and does and looks like, that any Earthling teen would endure.

Despite her quick and complete infatuation with Mark, however, Olwen is amazed that he and his fellow colonizers, unlike her, cannot stand the sun's rays and cannot tolerate Isis's thin, upper atmosphere.

They are all apparently weaklings and also, according to Guardian, possible disease carriers. Accordingly, Guardian fits Olwen with a suit and mask that he instructs her to never remove while visiting any of the colonizers, including Mark. Olwen consents, although she protests to Guardian:

> "You don't understand. I *love* Mark." It wasn't until she had actually said it that she realized that it was the truest and most important thing she had ever said. "I love Mark," she said again slowly. "I want him to see *me*. To get to know *me*." (70)

The *real me* is, of course, the issue and the surprise at the center of the novel. When Mark finally sees Olwen without her suit and mask (he tracks her unobserved to the top of a cliff), he is so startled he falls and is seriously injured. Olwen—along with us, the readers—then learns that Guardian, in an attempt to make her more resistant to Isis's not inconsiderable perils, has genetically altered her so that she is not vulnerable. ("'Isis is mine,' Olwen boasts early on to Mark, 'and it can never harm me in any way.'" 59). The problem is that this invulnerability also renders her, at least in appearance, not recognizably human. For her part, Olwen, who now realizes she has lived all her life in a house without mirrors and has never truly seen herself, is taken by surprise.

The reader and Olwen learn the truth: to protect her, Guardian gradually altered the human Olwen's bones, skin, and eyes and eyelids so that she can withstand the rigors of the deadly Isis. As the commander of the colonizers observes in a meeting with the unveiled Olwen:

> She looked like an exotic and intelligent lizard.... There was a dignified symmetry in the wide nose and heavy eyebrows.... The goldish-green of her skin was exotic, and even the nictating membrane, which he saw slide across her [blue] eyes in a sudden light reflection had a strange kind of fascination. (109)

Yet here Hughes may falter a bit, at least to some readers. Olwen—possibly reflecting her long-standing, unassailable sense of superiority—sees herself as certainly different but, examining herself in a mirror, also quickly concludes that Guardian has done a marvelous job and that she is "beautiful" (97). This conclusion is fortunate, as Guardian cannot, at this stage, change Olwen back, and soon her sense of self-assurance dominates her feelings for the earthling Mark.

Olwen now knows what she looks like—and she knows that it is not a human appearance. Further, as the novel moves swiftly to its climax, she realizes that Mark can probably never accept or love her. In another possibly damaging revelation, she also has learned from the colonizers' commander that her beloved Guardian is no more than a robot, a DaCoP Forty-Three who is designed for human service.

At the end, however, Olwen is undeterred and also heroic. Despite her youth, she saves an earthling child, gains the respect of the colonizers, forgives Mark for his cowardice, renounces his offer of love, and with Guardian decides to move higher into the Isis atmosphere so that she can be more useful to the colonizers. Hughes presents us with a triumph of self-abnegation over shame, sketching for the reader a wise Olwen. This is a young woman whose love and compassion confirm her humanity, her new strength and maturity, and her ability to live in contentment—not with her ostensible "kind," but with her beloved robot companion.

Among other themes, science fiction often addresses what it means to be human. As we earthlings exalt the glories of humanity, science fiction often holds up a mirror and asks us to consider extending that boundary to what is *other*. The extent to which aliens are human, the extent to which robots show human characteristics, the extent to which anyone from another planet or species can be human are perennial themes in science fiction literature and film.

The Keeper of the Isis Light is a superior book for consideration of what it means to be human. It is also, tangentially, about the loss of innocence. Olwen has no idea that her perfect body and perfect life, with which she is most pleased, are, to outsiders' eyes, both terribly flawed. She lives in a Garden of Eden; it is the colonizers and what they bring that are, for her, the Tree of Knowledge. When Olwen realizes the truth, however, she is initially hurt and confused, but she eventually triumphs and comes to reconsider what is important and useful and what is surface. While readers may disagree as to the convincing nature of Olwen's conclusions, Hughes asks us to believe her. And, if we do, Olwen tells us at the end of the novel that she is different but also, most importantly, mature and human in the truest sense of the term. Thinking of their future life together, she tells Guardian:

> "I love you. But I just realized something so sad. When I die, then *you* will be all alone. *You* will have no one."

"That is all right, Olwen. You must not be distressed. After all, I am not human. DaCoPs do not have the capacity to be lonely."

Olwen nodded and watched him walk stiffly across the living room to the kitchen.

"Poor Guardian," she whispered. (154)

BIBLIOGRAPHY

Hughes, Monica. *The Keeper of the Isis Light*. New York: Atheneum, 1981.
——. *The Guardian of Isis*. Toronto: Tundra Books, 1981.
——. *The Isis Pedlar*. Toronto: Tundra Books, 1982.
Sorenson, Marilou. "Monica Hughes." 141-48 in *Writers for Young Adults*, Vol. 2, ed. Ted Hipple. New York: Charles Scribner's Sons, 1997.

Leila Christenbury is a former high school English teacher who is currently professor of English education at Virginia Commonwealth University, Richmond, where she teaches young adult literature, English methods, and a seminar for student teachers. The former co-editor of *The ALAN Review* and the former editor of *English Journal*, she is president of the National Council of Teachers of English.

Chapter Fifteen

Two Forgotten Novels by Bruce Clements
Kenneth L. Donelson

Reviewers and critics have generally been kind to Bruce Clements, but his novels have never had the readers they deserved. That is especially true with two funny and often witty novels: *I Tell a Lie Every So Often* and *The Treasure of Plunderell Manor*.

I Tell a Lie Every So Often opens with one of the most striking paragraphs in young adult literature:

> I tell a lie every so often, and almost always nothing happens, but last spring I told a lie that carried me five hundred miles and made a lot of things happen. Somebody got shot because of it, and I had a visit with a beautiful naked girl who stood up in front of me early in the morning and talked in a foreign tongue, and I saw a ball game with a hundred men on one side and a hundred men and one girl on the other side, and a boat sank, somewhat, under me, and my brother Clayton started acting strangely and sleeping with a loaded rifle, and there are some more things, too. (5)

The time period of the story is 1850, and what fourteen-year-old Henry Desant says is true, though some of it is less dramatic in detail than it sounds in summary. Henry is never above lying, especially when it keeps him from doing something he doesn't want to—as when his stuffy brother, Clayton, is told by a presumably reputable source that Clayton's intended, Caroline Burke, pads her clothing, and Henry is sent to check Caroline's closet.

Henry decides that becoming a closet snoop isn't worth his time, and he lies to Clayton and reassures him that Caroline isn't stuffing any of her anatomy. Then, soon afterward, Henry tells Clayton another lie, this one more of a pure lie since "it wasn't about me. Lies about yourself are always vanity, and they hardly ever sound true" (12). This lie is that Henry has heard about a white girl with red hair who lives with Indians in the Dakota Territory. Since their cousin Hanna was taken by Indians a few years back and she was red-headed, Clayton and the family swallow Henry's lie and soon the two boys have left their St. Louis home and are heading west up the Missouri River.

Despite what the plot summary sounds like, the book is not primarily a tale of adventure and incident, but one of character. Clayton does not become less pompous, but he does become more believable, even human. Clements's ability to portray strange, Dickensian, frontier figures is a delight. Clayton admires The Rev. Basil Arthur Sweetvarnish who is writing a book, *The Lord's Divine Plan for America*. Titus Pewbrace's "life work is to spread joy and put aside ignorance among my neighbors." Henry is impressed with Pewbrace's size. "He was a tall man with a lumpy forehead and bushy eyebrows, so when he looked at you it was like being watched out of a tree" (62). The untrustworthy Mr. Hesterswine intrigues Henry because he tells more lies, for less noble motives, than Henry.

Some librarians and teachers have said that *I Tell a Lie Every So Often* is a special joy to read aloud, and they're right. It has the sound of a frontier tall-tale, a legend in the making, and the credit for that goes to Henry. Readers instinctively like him and believe in him, for he's a composite of off-beat traits mixed with a delightful ability to recognize human frailty—even his own—without becoming cocky or cynical or impossibly wise. He revels in his lies and invariably worries about their consequences, though that rarely stops him from yet another creative lie. Readers aren't taken in by him, but they can admire Henry's bigger-than-life imagination and wondrous execution.

For example, Henry's love of writing dreadful poetry loosely modeled after Shakespeare gets him into trouble early in the novel. Clytemnestra ("Clemmy") Burke, who replaced her sister in Clayton's heart, has recently fed snake meat to Henry in a meat pie. Henry, seeking revenge and inspiration, finds it in "A Sonnet Poem to Clemmy Burke, Purest Angel in the World" (18), which describes the effect of the snake meat on Henry, his sour stomach, and his vomiting on Clemmy's porch. Unfortunately, Henry's poetic language is so effective that Clemmy and Clayton alike are taken in by the poem and believe that Henry feels real passion (not an upset stomach) for Clemmy, something that Clayton never allows Henry to forget during their long journey to the West.

Richard Peck, himself an eminent novelist, praised Clements' work in a review in the Februrary 1975 issue of *American Libraries*, at the same time pointing out a problem, that the novel starts more promising than it finishes:

> A novelist with chutzpah essays Twain's own turn. A spunky, Missouri boy given to riverboat misadventures and mid-Victorian doggerel tells a shaggy-dog story with serious pretensions that falls apart at the end. But getting there is fun even if Clements isn't Clemens. (108)

The Treasure of Plunderell Manor is a far more successful novel, a wonderful spoof of Victorian gothic novels set in mid-Victorian England with one of the feistiest servant girl heroes in YA literature. It is not merely Clements's best book; it is a marvel of adventure and character and great humor and wit and one of the most delightful books in YA literature in many years.

We enter *Treasure* on a cold, muddy, most unpleasant day and watch fourteen-year-old Laurel Bybank trudge toward Plunderell Manor where she will become the maid of Alice Plunderell, soon to observe her eighteenth birthday. Before she reaches the manor, Laurel meets John Frame, former steward of the manor, who tells Laurel that Lord and Lady Stayne want Alice dead before her birthday to inherit the manor and the "hidden treasure." After the Staynes fired John, who is Alice's protector, he has lived in a cave under a tree. When Laurel asks John if he is a good man, John answers, "I don't know," and wonders why Laurel had asked. Laurel responds that her granny "used to tell me never to trust a man who thought he was good, and I want to trust you" (13). With that, Laurel captures our attention and affection and never loses either.

Her full name is easily explained. Her mother, too poor and ill to keep the child, left her in a basket tied to a laurel branch on the bank of the Trier River. She is an orphaned girl destined to rise in circumstances, and she does, the first in a series of conventions of the Gothic novel that Clements uses. Alice Plunderell, who we soon meet, is an heiress, fearfully alone and fearful of her life at the hands of her despicable and villainous guardians, Lord and Lady Stayne, who seek the hidden treasure that Alice will inherit on her eighteenth birthday. Alice can count on the friendship and loyalty of her estate's former steward, John Frame. Alice has her wealthy intended, Harold Pomfret-Watkin, to save her at the last moment. Names of things and people are significant in the Gothic tradition. The name, Plunderell Manor, has the cruel overtones of plunder and cruelty and is described as old and ugly. And the names of her guardians, Lord and Lady Stayne, have enough sinister overtones for any novel.

Clements obviously has fun with the Staynes, particularly the wonderful hypocrisy of Lord Stayne. When Laurel first meets him, he smiles at her with his "very brown teeth" and says, "I am a Good Christian man. And my dear Lady Stayne is the best of Christian Women," and compliments Laurel limply, "I can see that there is much goodness, of a sort, in you" (45). His purity and concern for Laurel is made clear only a few minutes later when he considers her religion.

> We must show concern ourselves with your soul, too. Catholics go to hell. From the Pope down. Just because you are simple and ignorant and weak, God will not forgive you for being a child of Rome. You may do as you wish, of course, but my advice is that you join the Anglican Church immediately. It's on your head, not mine. (52)

The Staynes know that they must do away with Alice and find the hidden treasure before Alice's eighteenth birthday. Lord Stayne takes Alice and Laurel to an abandoned monastery and leaves them to perish from starvation and cold. Death seems inevitable, but Laurel's ingenuity keeps the girls alive. When the villains are likely to return, the girls leave a trail to a nearby river to fool the Staynes into believing the girls have drowned.

Perhaps the funniest scene in *Treasure* comes when the Staynes believe the girls have drowned and begin their apparent victory celebration that soon turns into attempts to kill each other. Lady Stayne first draws blood by hitting Lord Stayne with a table leg and the battle is underway.

> There was blood running from his forehead and his left ear. "They're dead." He said. "They're drowned. You're trying to kill me. I insist that you cease."
>
> She sat on the ground, her face red and covered with sweat. "You are trying to put me in my grave," she said. "I will not have you give me an untimely death. Now, help me stand up."
>
> He helped her up, and she swung at him one more time. He swung back, hitting her on the side of her head. Her bonnet and wig flew high

into the air. It looked, for a moment, as if he had knocked her head off. She stood there, her ears sticking out. She was totally hairless, except for some black fuzz running across the top of her head from ear to ear. "For shame!" she screamed. "Fetch, fetch, fetch." (96)

At book's close and after the girls have gone to their own funerals, the treasure has been uncovered, the villains have been disposed of, and the romances of the young people have been straightened out, the conventions of the Gothic have been turned upside down as they must in a parody.

The fourteen-year-old Laurel has emerged as the hero of the book who has successfully managed the affairs of the now eighteen-year-old Alice. Alice remains a charming simple-minded child whose intended, Harold Pomfret-Watkin (of Watkin's soap and heir to a fortune) does nothing to help advance her cause or her life, though Alice would never have known and would care even less. John Frame, the simple but pure and loyal servant to Alice and Plunderell Manor gets Alice, though whether that's good is anyone's guess. And almost everyone, save the Staynes, but they are dead, is blissfully happy. Only Laurel, soon to travel to America, is unsure what lies ahead of her.

I Tell a Lie Every So Often and *The Treasure of Plunderell Manor* are satisfying books, mostly because of their attractive main characters and what they learn. Henry and Laurel learn that the world is rarely what it seems, full of appearances but often less substance. They learn that people are rarely totally trustworthy, especially when they are totally human. They learn that when life seems to be unravelling, they are part of that rare breed of people who can restore the cloth and make it whole and give it meaning. They learn that being survivors means helping others to survive as well. And they learn that their common sense and sense of humor may be the two best senses of all.

A PUZZLED END NOTE

I love humor, but I've long been puzzled about why the five YA novels that have most amused me over the years have often gone virtually unnoticed. That may be hyperbole, but not too much so. Here are my five favorites: (1) Leon Garfield's *The Strange Affair of Adelaide Harris*. A spoof of legends and romances and love intrigues that make up many eighteenth-century novels; (2) John Townsend's *Kate and the Revolution*. A spoof of court intrigue in the tradition of Anthony Hope's *The Prisoner of Zenda*; (3) Judie Angell's *Suds*, a spoof of soap opera, and life, too, for that matter; (4) Robert Kaplow's *Alex Icicle: A Romance in Ten Torrid Chapters*. A spoof of horror stories and Edgar Allan Poe; and (5) Bruce Clements' *The Treasure of Plunderell Manor*. A spoof of Gothic thrillers.

A possible, if nasty, theory to account for the lack of attention to the few YA novels that are intentionally humorous is that most of us (English teachers and librarians) take pride in taking life seriously. God knows life is grim and serious most of the time, so we may find less significance, less importance, in books that are funny, books that seem intent on making us forget the seriousness of life. But there's always time for comedy, especially in the most serious of times, which is always now. I've always admired the opening line of Rafael Sabatini's 1921 tale of the French Revolution, *Scaramouche*: "He was born with a gift of laughter and a sense that the world was mad." More of us ought to remember that line. Maybe we might even act as if it had truth.

BIBLIOGRAPHY

Angell, Judie. *Suds*. New York: Bradbury, 1983.
Clements, Bruce. *I Tell a Lie Every So Often*. New York: Farrar Straus and Giroux, 1974.
———. *The Treasure of Plunderell Manor*. New York: Farrar Straus and Giroux, 1987.
Garfield, Leon. *The Strange Affair of Adelaide Harris*. New York: Pantheon, 1971.
Kaplow, Robert. *Alex Icicle: A Romance in Ten Torrid Chapters*. Boston: Houghton Mifflin, 1984.
Townsend, John. *Kate and the Revolution*. New York: Lippincott, 1982.

Ken Donelson is director of the English education program at Arizona State University where he has taught since 1965. Before earning his Ph.D. with G. Robert Carlson at the University of Iowa, he taught in high schools and became interested in censorship. He is co-author with Alleen Pace Nilsen of the textbook *Literature for Today's Young Adults*.

Chapter Sixteen

Aidan Chambers's *Breaktime:* A Lost Masterwork by a Found Master Craftsman

Ted Hipple

"Literature is crap." So ends chapter one of Aidan Chambers's first novel for young adults, *Breaktime*. Published in 1978 but now out of print in the United States, this work nonetheless marked—and, for new readers, continues to mark—Chambers as one of the premier writers of fiction for adolescents, an accolade that has increased with his later books. As I commented in an entry in *Writers for Young Adults* (Scribners, 1997), Chambers is a "master wordsmith, a writer whose affection for language—its sounds and shapes and meanings, its awesome variety and amazing versatility" (219) is everywhere apparent whenever he puts pen to paper. Hence, it may be appropriate to begin with a bit about the life of the man.

Born in a small English town in 1934, Aidan lived a relatively lonely life for much of his youth, with few close "mates," as the British would put it. He followed solitary pursuits, like going to the movies and to local dramatic productions, and read widely, though not necessarily for school assignments. In fact, he did not do well in school, mostly because of boredom. He did develop a fondness and admiration for some of his teachers, among them Jim Osborne, whom he encountered when Aidan's family moved to the larger town of Darlington. Osborne recognized Aidan's considerable talents, particularly with language, and insisted that he join the school's debate and drama clubs. It was a good beginning for the young Aidan, intellectually and socially. (Interestingly, a character named Jim Osborne appears in a later novel, *Dance on My Grave*, as an especially sensitive teacher.)

After a stint in the navy, Chambers returned to college and became a secondary school teacher; he also renewed what became a lifelong study of religion. So important was this subject to Chambers that he helped found a monastery, one of whose major purposes was to provide guidance for troubled youth. But while there he continued to teach part time and also to edit the writings of colleagues and to write himself. After seven years in the monastery he faced a difficult choice: monk? teacher? editor? writer? Happily for those interested in novels that have both appeal and serious meanings for young adults, he selected the life of an author.

Breaktime became the first of a planned sextet of novels about youth, though not in a sequel-sense of continuing characters and settings and plot lines. Rather, Chambers's novels would explore differing facets of adolescent life. To date, four more of these six—with *Breaktime*, five in all—have appeared and received much acclaim. The second was *Dance on My Grave* (1982), which dealt with emotions, particularly alternative kinds of love and obsession; N.I.K.: *Now I Know* (1987), with spiritual experience; *The Toll Bridge* (1992), with introspection and depression, what its protagonist calls "the glums"; and *Postcards from No Man's Land* (2000), with cultural and generational differences. While not all of these are still in print in the United States, they remain critically and commercially popular in most other parts of the English-speaking world.

What is special about the first of the sextet, *Breaktime*? Careful readers of the novel will provide a variety of answers, but it seems likely that their judgments can be subsumed under three headings—compelling story, meaningful exploration of themes important to young adults, and fascinating use of language and other symbols.

First the story. The protagonist Ditto (and why that name? stereotypical adolescent? chip off the fatherly block?) and his best friend Morgan, both seventeen, love the debates and discussions that surround their young lives, some of them rooted in sexual matters (Morgan is experienced; Ditto is a virgin), others in schoolhouse issues, like the meaning of literature. It is Morgan who avers that "literature is crap," among other charges against the subject. Ditto loves literature and agrees to provide a counter argument.

At the same time, life at home for Ditto has taken a bad turn. An only child, he and his newly crippled and bitter-about-it father can no longer talk about anything at all without becoming angry and ugly. When his father suffers a mild heart attack during one of their verbal back-and-forths, Ditto feels guilty and decides to go away for a few days during a school break. His goals are mixed: distance from his father, a chance to prepare a written argument for Morgan that will take the form of a story and provide rebuttal for their debate, and, most important of all, an opportunity to meet with the delectable Helen, from whom comes the promise of sex. An earlier friend who moved away, Helen had recently begun a provocative correspondence.

Ditto travels only a short distance, but it is enough. While away, he first meets Jack and Robbie, two wild youth who drink too much beer with him, engage him in a union meeting where Robbie's father is the principal speaker, a meeting that they riotously disrupt, and, worst of all, enlist his support for breaking into a house and robbing it. During the burglary, Ditto is a latter-day Oliver Twist who climbs through a window to open the back door. (Chambers actually includes an extensive quote from the Dickens novel.) As it turns out, the house is the home of Robbie's wealthy father, from whom the son is estranged, and who discovers all three in their crime. Recognizing that Ditto barely knows what is occurring, the father lets him leave without alerting the police. And the next day Ditto does meet Helen. Ditto writes of all of his experiences, including, when he returns home, an easing of the tension between him and his father, and presents the account to Morgan as evidence that literature is—can be, at least something—other than crap. What Morgan does not know is how much of Ditto's novel is true, how much made up. And Ditto refuses to tell him. The novel ends with Morgan, having read the whole of what Ditto wrote and discovering he is a part of it, being puzzled: "I'm in the thing," Morgan said. "Are you saying I'm just a character in a story?" "Aren't we all?" said Ditto and laughed (180).

The themes in *Breaktime* cut across many aspects of adolescent life: relationships with peers and with family, sex, school, alienation, and, perhaps most pivotal of all, self-knowledge. Ditto, not the most popular of boys, has a good relationship with Morgan, with the two rowdies he meets, and finally with Helen. These relationships give clear indication that he can respond and be responded to. Though the instructor never appears in the novel, Ditto often comments on his literature teacher Midgely ("Midge"), with whom he has a kind of mutual admiration society.

But with his family Ditto faces strained relationships. He and his father are oil and water; separately they are all right, but they don't mix well. And his poor mother, exhausted from having to return to work at a menial job to keep the family above the abject poverty level and, at the same time, referee the squabbles at home, engenders a depressing sense in Ditto that he is a major cause of the family's lack of respect and tolerance. What to do? His unlettered father calls Ditto a "twit" because he loves Jane Austen, "some dead woman writer." And then Ditto, no more mature, reacts with a similar disparagement and the two, father and son, are off and running once again, emotionally head-on at each other.

Among teenagers, relationships like these with peers and with family are not at all uncommon. Chambers, well aware of the proverb that suggests that "the existence of a problem does not imply the existence of a solution," offers no easy panaceas for Ditto's malaise at home. But neither is the author totally bleak. At the end of the novel there appears at least the glimmer of a rapprochement on the family front and a hope that life may be better.

Both school and sex are significant in Ditto's life, just as they are in the lives of virtually all adolescents. And in those realms Ditto is successful, intellectually and physically. Putting aside his father's nastiness about his love of literature, Ditto appears to earn the respect of his teachers and of his good friend and mental equal, Morgan. His planned meeting with Helen works, in fact, as planned; she is experienced, he inexperienced but eager to be taught. Clearly Chambers is cognizant of the importance of sex and school and tolerant of the uncertainties, frustrations, feelings of guilt, and emotional highs and lows that accompany the thoughts and actions associated with classrooms and—teens hope—bedrooms.

The commentary about alienation in *Breaktime* appears mostly in the scenes with the two young and loutish companions Ditto hooks up with on his trip. Jack is a drifter, away from wherever his home is and temporarily bonded with current friend Robbie, whose angst about his father's hypocritical political views—exceedingly rich, the "old sod" still preaches about the virtues of socialism—colors his every judgment and action. When Ditto realizes Robbie and Jack withheld from him the fact that the burglarized house belonged to Robbie's father, Ditto decides he's had enough of the bitterness and the mean-spirited and stupid reactions of Jack and Robbie and he leaves them, to await the elegant Helen, due to arrive the next day.

Helen and Ditto do have sex and the activity, long sought, often imagined, but never actually experienced by Ditto, adds considerably to his store of self-information. He is in retrospect somewhat analytical about the act. He was, he knows, decent about it all, treating Helen kindly, not as the "easy lay" she uses to describe herself. And she, too, is grateful. Even though they will probably never meet again, Ditto now is privy to a few of the secrets of intimacy and has come nearer to being the sexual equal of the more worldly Morgan.

Ditto also gleans information about himself when, at the end of the novel, he receives a gift from his father, two trophies the latter had earned for his teenaged prowess in motorcycle racing. Ditto knows that he earlier would have disdained the gift, possibly even refused it, but now he understands, even a bit tearfully, that his love for his father is real and their disagreements must be bridged, something his father also seems willing to try.

Plot and themes notwithstanding, for many readers it is Chambers's extraordinary ability with language that most captures their enthusiasm. With all the skill and finesse of a circus lion tamer, Chambers plays with language, at once teasing it (and the reader), next making it move through hurdles of his own design, then being totally straightforward in his approach. For example, Ditto's adventures are sometimes described in first person—he is, after all, writing a story to be used to counter Morgan's argument that "literature is crap"—but in parallel descriptions Chambers uses third-person narration. An obvious fan of the Mark Twain dictum that "the difference between the right word and the almost right word is like the difference between lightning and the lightning bug," Chambers, in all of his novels, frequently sends readers to the dictionary for the definition of that right, and highly unusual, word. Two such instances in *Breaktime* are "dissentient" and "epulation." Chambers frequently switches the size or font of letters, sometimes even within a single sentence, but not in a show-off way; their use adds to whatever he is talking about at that moment.

Moreover, Chambers uses symbols and word and line arrangements to make more graphic what he writes about even more graphic. In the riot scene at the union hall, the speaker puts his audience to sleep as he drones on and seems barely able to stay awake himself. Chamber's devotes an entire page to an outline of a man's face, done all in tiny Z's, and what comes out of wide-open mouth but another string of Z's. Later at that same meeting, when Robbie and Jack and Ditto create a ruckus, Ditto is popped on the nose; another full page shows a fist coming directly at the reader, behind which appear in bold the shouted words "OUT! OUT!" In the sexual intercourse description Chambers uses both first and third person to describe Ditto and Helen's behavior and his reactions to it, putting them in alternate lines, one of them italicized—but on only one column on each page; a second column contains the textbook description of sex found in a book by Dr. Spock. As in:

She shifted her position, so that *Don't talk she says, but the mind* she could undo the buttons of my *goes on. Why won't it stop? Give up.* shirt, which she accomplished slowly, *Give up itself to what is happening?*	There is not much point in trying to describe lovemaking— whether it is hand holding, embracing, fondling, or intercourse. (158)

This kind of artistry continues for four full pages and is representative of the creative use of language and symbol that appear throughout the book. For those even mildly interested in language, the appeal of *Breaktime* is almost irresistible.

Breaktime is one of those "lost" books, at least to American teenagers, and that is sad. Let us hope that, as more young adults find the novel, it can regain the attention it and its author so richly deserve.

BIBLIOGRAPHY

Chambers, Aidan. *Breaktime*. New York: HarperCollins, 1978.
Hipple, Ted. "Aiden Chambers." 219-27 in *Writers for Young Adults*, vol. 1, edited by Ted Hipple. New York: Scribners's Sons, 1997.

Ted Hipple is professor of English education at the University of Tennessee. Active in NCTE, he has chaired the Conference on English Education, the Secondary Section of the Council, was one of the founders of ALAN, and served that organization as its president and executive secretary. He was written widely about English education and adolescent literature and edited Scribner's four-volume work on *Writers for Young Adults*.

Chapter Seventeen

About Living On: *Sheila's Dying* by Alden Carter

Pam Muñoz Ryan

I knew that Sheila and I were finished. And it wasn't just because she hadn't made love to me. Somehow we just weren't very happy together anymore. Ya, it was over. All we had to do was make it official.

I had no idea what a bitch that would be. (81)

In Alden R. Carter's trenchant novel, *Sheila's Dying*, high school junior, Jerry Kincaid, decides to break up with his girlfriend, Sheila. But before he tells her that their relationship is over, she gets violently ill and the doctor discovers that she has a rare form of cancer with no known treatment. Jerry is a responsible, serious teenager with a strong sense of obligation to his mother and sister (his father left the family years before). Bound by moral duty, he feels he must not abandon Sheila. His life becomes cluttered with the conflicts between his family, studies, and basketball, Sheila's physically demanding condition, and her emotional premise that they are still boyfriend and girlfriend. Jerry, along with his high school nemesis, Bonnie, who is Sheila's only other close friend, tackle the unfamiliar journey of caring for someone facing the inevitable.

When Alden Carter was asked about why he wrote *Sheila's Dying*, he said,

> I was interested in writing a novel about teenage relationships and was musing on how difficult they can be even under ordinary circumstances. That led me to thinking about extraordinary circumstances. . . . I felt the plot would give me an opportunity to explore the theme of relationships and the major theme of virtually all young adult novels: the process of maturing. (e-mail correspondence, derived from a prepared list of answers to frequently-asked questions)

The main character matures, admirably. Here is a story about the human condition and friendship that reaches beyond romantic or sexual love. Unlike trite stories of athletes whose skills get better during the emotional turmoil of their lives and go on to win the big game for the ailing person, Jerry's basketball prowess diminishes, and he is cut from the team. My affection for this book is that Alden Carter doesn't give the reader the pat and the predictable. He gives the reader a strong slap of reality. Smack. Right in the face. Cope, Jerry. Struggle. Mature.

The language is blunt and in context. Smoking and drinking abound but solicit a verity that young adults will recognize. Although cast in 1987 and the characters use the words "going steady" to refer to their relationship, the dialogue is otherwise contemporary, and the minor dating of words doesn't impact the strengths of the novel. Opportunities for discussion are plentiful. This book begs to illicit reader responses about the issues of sexual love versus emotional love, sports, duty, and death. It is gratefully, not a romantic tragedy that would pander to sentimentality and mediocrity. Instead, it is death and life in living color.

Carter presents an array of characters with different reactions to Sheila's demise and the possibility of death in general. Mike, the Indian, is spiritual and a loyal friend. Sheila's grandmother copes through alcohol. Jerry and Bonnie cope with a sense of purpose and caregiving. And then there is Phil, who won't come to visit Sheila because he "just can't think about death," (199). Again, these presentations provide fodder for readers to discuss, write about, and examine their own feelings and probable reactions.

Among the many awards and noted lists for *Sheila's Dying* were an ALA Best Book for Young Adults, New York Library Best Book for the Teenage, Los Angeles Public Library Best Book for Young Adults, and an ALA Best Book for Reluctant Readers. The awards, honors, and teen appeal were apparent. So, why did *Sheila's Dying* go out of print?

After a phone interview with Refna Wilkin, the editor of *Sheila's Dying*, I learned that the hardcover sales were not enough to justify keeping the book in print, especially a book that then (over ten years ago) was on the upper end of the young adult age range. She felt that today, with the resurgence of young adult literature in recent years, *Sheila's Dying* might be embraced by a broader audience. I felt that the title might have been one of the factors. Alden Carter reported that Sheila is not the main character. Jerry and Bonnie come before her in his priority, yet the title features her name. The book is more about how the characters that surround Sheila cope with her death and the continuum of life. In addition, there is always hesitancy by some people to read about death. When I asked Refna if the title had ever been an issue, she admitted that there had been considerable discussion about the title before publication, but that she fought for the title. She emphasized that although Sheila was not the main character, she was the catalyst of the story. Certainly, recasting *Sheila's Dying* with another title and a more contemporary cover could be a consideration.

Curious about the author's thoughts on this novel, I contacted Alden Carter. Many students and teachers have written to him about their revelations and epiphanies after reading this book. Alden Carter said,

> My imagination has been a lot of places since I wrote *Sheila's Dying,* but it remains a book close to my heart. For me, it's always been a story not about death but about living on. By being with Sheila in her dying, Jerry and Bonnie receive one of life's great gifts: a sense of their own mortality. In some ways perhaps childhood ends when we realize that our lives are not unbounded, that we should savor our days, try to be useful, try to be kind. I think Jerry and Bonnie come to realize something of this. From the mail I've received over the years, some young readers have found the book useful in their search for maturity. I'm proud of that. And grateful. (e-mail correspondence)

I found the book intriguing and compelling. I wanted to turn the pages and was often surprised at Carter's ability to surprise me with directness and confrontation. *Sheila's Dying* is thought-provoking. And for me and the young adults I know, that at the very least, continues to make this book a worthy read.

BIBLIOGRAPHY

Carter, Alden R. *Sheila's Dying*. New York, NY: G. P. Putnam's Sons, 1987.

Pam Muñoz Ryan, a former teacher and administrator, is now a full-time writer who has written books for adults, picture books for young children, and books for older readers. Her award-winning books include *Esperanza Rising*, a 2001 ALA Top Ten Best Book and recipient of the Pura Belpre Award, and *Riding Freedom*, the winner of the 1999–2000 California Young Readers Medal. She lives north of San Diego, California, with her husband and four children.

Chapter Eighteen

Send No Blessings and *The Year of the Gopher:* Phyllis Reynolds Naylor's Lost Masterpieces about Setting One's Own Course

Lois T. Stover

Every year during advising sessions I talk with my undergraduate students, all of whom are future teachers, about their academic progress. Often, I receive one of the following two responses. Sometimes a student will sigh and shake her head sadly, saying she is still getting pressure from her parents to withdraw from the certification program, to head for a job at the local naval base in which she can use her degree from our "honors college" to earn an income significantly higher than she would make as a teacher. Her parents, she will say, just do not appreciate that she wants to serve the greater good in some capacity. At other times, the student might tell me she is getting pressure from her family to return to a less demanding schedule, to stop taking classes and focus more on her spouse and children, who need her. After all, her husband earns enough to care for the family financially, and nobody in the family has ever felt the need to go to college before now. Members of her family, she will say, do not appreciate that she wants an intellectual challenge, that she wants to continue to learn and grow in the process.

In both cases, my students are having difficulty being true to themselves in the face of certain family values that clash with their own. This tension is central in two now out-of-print titles by Phyllis Reynolds Naylor, *Send No Blessings* (1990) and *The Year of the Gopher* (1987). These books are important to "rescue" because each features a high school senior striving to develop an independent identity in the face of realistically described and all-too-common family pressures. I like this pairing of titles because both books deal with the same thematic issues, albeit in two quite different family settings. *Send No Blessings*, is about a young girl, Beth, from a rural community in which education is not valued. Her large, sprawling family depends on her, as the oldest child, to help with the younger ones—and they are looking forward to her graduation from high school because then she can work and contribute to the family's well being, even if she marries the young man they all admire who drives the bread delivery truck. *The Year of the Gopher* is about a young man, George, who comes from a long line of lawyers. Naturally, he will go to an Ivy League school and become an attorney in the family firm. George, too, is the oldest child in the family. He is expected to set the example for his younger siblings and to shoulder responsibility for continuing the family traditions. Naylor's titles deserve to be resurrected because they explore a crucial fact of life for older adolescents: the need to determine individual strengths, commitments, and values in the midst of limiting family structures.

Additionally, both of these titles show Naylor at her literary best. The tensions between Beth and George and their families come alive because of Naylor's skill in character development, particularly through dialogue and interior monologue that beautifully capture the sense of being torn. At one point, George's father takes George on a disastrous tour of East Coast colleges. While George knows his father cares about him, he comes to realize that his father knows very little about him. He thinks to himself,

> I regret that I have but one life to give for my father . . . I felt miserable, but something told me that if I didn't stand up to him now, I'd be lost. If I let him put me on the old railroad, I'd never get off, and before you knew it, Jess and Ollie would be on it, too. Somebody had to look out for them, especially for Ollie. (*Gopher,* 42-43)

George is incensed when he discovers that his parents think Ollie, his younger brother, does not care about school, does not care that his difficulties with learning disappoint them. Nor can he believe that his father thinks he, himself, has no worries; George tells us that he has lived with chronic anxiety since he was four, trying to meet his parents' expectations. He finally realizes that his parents *need* successful children. In many ways, they feel their own success as parents is based on whether or not the accomplishments of their children can make them proud. George also recognizes that his parents themselves were the products of similar home environments, and he becomes determined to break the chain. He sabotages all his college applications, and rejection letters start to pour into the house. When his mother confronts him, George finally has the courage to tell her,

> I said it every way I knew how, but you weren't listening.... You don't care about me, you don't care about my education, you only care about how it makes you *look*... Somebody had to make the break. I'm not going to end up at an Ivy League school with a bottle of Maalox just to please you and Dad. (*Gopher*, 75-76)

As the remainder of the novel unfolds, we see George accepting responsibility for his actions. He takes a job as a bicycle messenger, learns more about many different kinds of people, and develops a friendship with a young woman based on mutual liking and respect. He also reaches out to his siblings, and, in the end, he decides his own future course of action: he will go to the University of Minnesota, in his home town, to become a school guidance counselor.

Another interesting aspect of this novel is that, as George takes the initiative to break patterns of behavior long-established in his family, the rest of them begin to grow and develop as well. His mother realizes that she does not, in fact, want to move out of her classroom and into administration. The money and prestige may be higher for a principal, but she recognizes that she *loves* teaching and does not want to move away from her students. Mr. Richards, George's father, is, in the end, impressed with the way George accepts responsibility on the job. He comes to admire how George budgets his time and money, and how he uses his "gophering" year to take stock of what matters to him. As a result, he offers George a new bike, one more appropriate for George as he rides through Minnesota streets in the winter. He is even able to say that the world probably has more than enough lawyers, letting George know he accepts his career decision.

In this novel, Naylor provides young adults with a realistic model of what it means to challenge the status quo within one's family. The tensions are finely wrought, and George's life as a "gopher" is not easy. But George's journey toward selfhood and independence, which form the basis for the action of the plot, provide, as a review in *Booklist* notes, "a welcome antidote to the compulsive, driving, college-entrance pressure exemplified in many nonfiction books" (1108). Steve Matthews, writing in *School Library Journal*, states that Naylor's gift is that she "stops just short of patness and reaffirms the complexity and pain of coming of age" (116). Although the book has been listed as "out of print" since 1993, the story, and George's strong male voice, the situations in which he finds himself, and the tensions he faces, all make this novel one well worth reading by adolescents a decade later.

Beth Herndon in *Send No Blessings* is similar to George in that she is desperate to find a way to pull away from her family and chart her own course through life. But she comes from very different circumstances: her parents are members of the rural poor, housing a family of ten in a double-wide trailer outside a small town in West Virginia. It is a loving family and Beth is relatively happy with her lot, until she starts high school and hears the other kids on the school bus expressing disbelief that people could live as she and her family do. At that moment, Naylor uses description of the physical setting to illuminate a change of perspective on the part of the character. Beth reflects on the fact that she always felt the trailer in its setting to be very pretty and serene, nestled near a river and below the sheltering mountains. Now, however, her eyes

> focused on the Crisco can holding up one corner of the dilapidated porch her father had built . . . the old refrigerator standing outside in the rain . . . the torn sheets of plastic over the windows.
>
> [Now she can] hear what she had tuned out before . . . feel the kinds of things that made her silent now around the house. Her own little world at the foot of the cliff had developed a crack, and others were looking in. (*Blessings*, 5–6)

Shortly thereafter, Beth overhears her father telling her mother that the manager of the local diner is willing to hire Beth as a full-time waitress once she turns sixteen and can leave school. Beth carves the word "not" into her school notebook, underscoring her determination not to leave school early, but she knows the obstacles she will face. She imagines her father yelling, "You saying no to me, girl?" and knows that somehow she will "have to get up the courage to say yes" (*Blessings*, 17). Unfortunately, unlike George, Beth is not a natural student, and the fact that she puts in late nights making artificial flowers and caring for her younger siblings make it hard for her to study. She discovers that she has a natural gift for typing, however, and she throws herself into improving her spelling and composing skills in an effort to please her typing teachers. As a result of both her efforts and her facility on the keyboard, the teachers award her an unsolicited scholarship to a three-week career-planning seminar hosted at the state university. Beth confronts her father and wins grudging approval from him for her adventure. She then sets off to take advantage of this unexpected gift, knowing her life will never be the same. While the Herndon family members do not engage in the same sort of parallel reflection and growth that George's family experiences, they do set Beth free to find a different path through life than the one to which they have been restricted.

The tensions between Beth and her parents, particularly with her father, the descriptions of life in rural poverty, and the "painful honesty" of Beth's struggles to define herself won this novel a place on *Booklist's* "Best Books for Young Adults" list for 1991. It remains well worth reading today because of its additional themes of hard work leading to success, a child's longing for adult recognition, and a young woman seeking to develop an identity not dependent on being in a relationship with a man. Naylor has an excellent ear for dialogue and can focus on thematic issues of universal importance to older adolescents without resorting to violence or extreme situations. These two novels should not remain "lost" but should be available for readers to enjoy today.

BIBLIOGRAPHY

"Best Books for Young Adults in 1991." *Booklist* 87. (15 March, 1991): 1478.
Matthews, Steve. "The Year of the Gopher." *School Library Journal,* 33 (May, 1987): 116.
Naylor, Phyllis Reynolds. *Send No Blessings*. New York: Atheneum, 1990.
———. *The Year of the Gopher*. New York: Atheneum, 1987.
"The Year of the Gopher." *Booklist* 83. (1 March, 1981): 1008.

Lois Stover, chair of educational studies at St. Mary's College of Maryland, teaches courses in educational psychology, pedagogical strategies, and children's and young adult literature. She is a former high school and middle school English and drama teacher, and the mother of an adolescent girl who loves Naylor's Alice series.

Chapter Nineteen

Finding One's Place in the World: *The Catalogue of the Universe* by Margaret Mahy

Patricia P. Kelly

My first introduction to Margaret Mahy's novels was through her book *Memory*. I was struck by her use of metaphorical language, her sensitive development of characters, and her ability to create a story that transcended its New Zealand setting. I subsequently read all her other young adult novels and was especially captivated by *The Catalogue of the Universe*. It is there that I found mythical Dido May (Mahy gives Dido her own maiden name), who scythes her lawn by moonlight, who lives in a dreamlike reality, and who fiercely protects her daughter, Angela, from the truth about her father. Mahy says that *The Catalogue of the Universe* is her favorite book and that she has a "bit in common" with Dido because she used to drive over the hill to work with her daughters, having meaningful discussions on the way, much as Dido and Angela do (*Writers for Young Adults*, 315).

Dido, an unmarried mother, has wanted Angela to grow up feeling loved and wanted. Dido has, therefore, spun stories of the love and sacrifice that Angela's father has made for them. Angela, however, locates her father and confronts him, only to discover the disdain he has always had for both Dido and his child. Devastated by his cold rejection, her confidence shaken, Angela turns to her best friend, Tycho Potter, for comfort. Tycho is a quirky, intellectual guy who sometimes wonders why popular, beautiful, and sensuous Angela wants to spend time with him. Tycho's family wonders the same thing. But Angela and Tycho, high school seniors, talk about the universe and philosophy and families and love. The novel's complexity, though, lies in the depth of the interpersonal relationships, in the intertextualities layered throughout, and in the magic realism lightly embedded in unexpected ways. These combined features enhance the literary value of this "lost masterpiece."

One of the major characteristics in all Mahy's young adult novels is her varied portraits of family relationships. *The Catalogue of the Universe* is a story of four families, none of them typical. Two of the families are drawn in detail, and though both are loving, they serve as counterpoint. Two others are drawn in lesser detail and reflect homes devoid of love.

Dido May has, through hard work and sacrifice, fashioned a home on a mountainside outside the city, " a cottage where nobody else wanted to live" (176), a house that fit Dido's feelings about herself at the time—"not good enough" (175). The outside bathroom and perilous road are a source of irritation to her daughter Angela, as is Dido's tenuous hold on reality. Though fanciful and dreamy, Dido has devoted her life to making Angela feel special, a child born of love. Dido has struggled alone, shielding Angela from the raw truth about her father and his mother who controlled him, ordered Dido from the house, and gave her money for an abortion. In many ways, Dido's small family is a triumph against evil.

On the other hand, the members of Tycho Potter's family seem unable to cope with the demands of life. Left disabled by an accident, his father is a good, well-meaning man. Though his mother loves and cares for her family, she is somewhat intimidated by them and fearful of the world outside. Tycho's older brother Richard, unkempt in junk-store clothes, wants to be a playwright but mostly lies around the house being disagreeable. And Africa, a married sister, adds to the family chaos when her own marriage falters. Amid the disorder in his family, Tycho, the youngest, is mostly left alone to study his books and contemplate the order of nature. The Potters are a wrangling, loud family, but Mrs. Potter longs for loveliness and peace. Still hopeful, she has tried her whole life to make other people happy.

Rich and distantly cold, the Chase family is the antithesis of Dido's family and the Potter family. Handsome and cruel, Roland Chase coolly rejects his daughter Angela, saying that he had "never ever been remotely curious" (92) about her. Unwilling to accept any responsibility for the direction his life has taken, he bitterly lashes out at his mother, Angela Chase, when she recognizes her granddaughter and namesake. Mrs. Chase has controlled the direction of her son's life but cannot now change the unhappy course of events. At that meeting and later, when Mrs. Chase again tries to establish a relationship, Angela refuses because she knows that to do so would be a rejection of everything her mother had given her.

Entirely different from the others, the fourth family relationship has barely begun before it is tragically betrayed. Africa, Mrs. Potter's daughter, is irresponsible and selfish. Each time she argues with her husband, she comes back to the Potter home with her son. Eventually she falls for a university professor; her first wedding anniversary breaks into a screaming match; and she brings her son home for the grandparents to fight over for custody. Blithely Africa says, "I don't mind admitting failure . . . it sets you free to do better" (163), but in the meantime she has wreaked havoc on the lives of those around her.

A different type of literary element in the novel is the interweaving of texts within a text, a technique known as intertextuality. Such layering of other genres within a story deepens its complexity. For example, Dido, the queen of Carthage in Roman mythology, is Dido May's namesake. Myth, also, is the text that Dido has created to protect her child from the hurts of illegitimacy: the myth, the fairy story, that Angela was a child of love, that her father sacrificed his own happiness for the good of his wife and three children, and that he provided for Dido and Angela all that he could give. In truth, Angela is enveloped in Dido's unselfish love and moral courage. Angela has her father's handsome looks, but she has Dido's strength to tell her father, "[W]e've faced the storm and won as ourselves. We've been fine. I've never needed a father. I was just curious" (92). Angela realizes that, in truth, she is a child of love, her mother's love. Myth becomes reality.

Another layer of a different text is the "Ionian idea that existence might be made understandable, even predictable, because it has an inner order that could be discovered and understood" (115). According to this Greek philosophy, life is rational, but little in Tycho's and Angela's lives is rational. Angela searches for her identity by confronting her father and instead rediscovers her mother. Tycho regrets his "otherness" but learns to value his intellect and difference through Angela's love. Both learn that love, like the square root of two, is not rational and, therefore, love must be governed by non-Ionian principles.

The Catalogue of the Universe, a book given to Tycho as a birthday present by Angela, is also a text that becomes the focal point of their discussions. They piece together tidbits of information, trying to make sense of the universe and their lives. Tycho knows that both a crater on the moon and a star were named for Tycho, the scientist, but learns that his mother offhandedly picked the name from a magazine in the doctor's office, thus plugging his "head into an infinite system" (112) based on a random textual encounter.

Tycho's brother, Richard, is an aspiring playwright, and the text that he should write is the scene where Tycho comes home a hero, but the family is in the chaos of Africa's return so they hardly notice him. In another textual reference, Tycho paraphrases Shakespeare, "Events are the stuff of the world and each of them is of brief duration" (166), and thus writes the prologue for his homecoming and television interview. Yet another type of text is interspersed throughout the scene as Tycho's thoughts play out as commercials for retail products.

Another literary feature of the novel is magic realism. Exemplified in the works of Garcia Márquez, Italo Calvino, and others, magic realism is a mixture of realism and fantasy. It is an imaginative way of thinking, a blend of romanticism, surrealism, and rationalism (Rincón, 178). The characters associated with magic realism in the novel are Dido and Tycho. When the mythical and fanciful Dido scythes the lawn by moonlight, her head seems "to leak moonshine" (46). One weekend for no reason but to brighten their lives she dyes everything in the house, and the delicious new colors "danced against the blue sky"(90) on the clothes line high atop their mountain. Ethereal and other-worldly, Dido, "a fairy-tale woman" (4), lives in her home in the air.

Tycho's imagination blends fantasy and realism. Tycho's mind is grounded in facts about the universe, but his imagination takes everything one step beyond reality. He knows that "common sense and truth don't match" and that common sense has a sort of symmetry, "whereas actual truth wobbles" (44) because truth lacks symmetry. For Tycho, love wobbles, and he feels "the wobble in the heart of the world as a great hesitation in the solid existence of chairs and tables, and men and women too" (55). While walking with Angela one day, Tycho sees "one cloud open an eye and look at him" (42). He has imaginary conversations with people like a tailor who is fitting him for clothes, "pinning him up in some new hopes" (160). When Tycho says he'll not "bother with the fears," the tailor says he "can't really have one without the other. . . . They're coordinated" (160). In other words, hope and fear go together. At the end, thinking of the two days' events, Tycho sees "light and dark, sun and stars, the air roared with traffic, rustled with hedgehogs . . . [he] felt himself actually become the catalogue of the universe, never finished, always being added to" (184–185).

Well known for numerous children's books, Mahy has written a few young adult novels, but only three that would appeal to older teens— *The Changeover*, *Memory*, and *The Catalogue of the Universe*. Her reputation as a children's writer may account for the current "lost" status of *The Catalogue of the Universe*, despite the depth of its literary quality. With both female and male protagonists, the book is equally Angela's and Tycho's story; in fact, the chapters for the most part alternate between the two. Tycho sees himself as a misfit in a world that focuses on appearance. Though lovely on the outside, Angela also feels her otherness because of her home and her illegitimacy. It is a novel with a universal theme: the search for self and for one's place in the world.

The value of the novel also lies in its rich language and complex structure. Vivid, almost poetic descriptions filled with allusions are characteristic of Mahy's writing. However, it is the intertextualities and elements of magic realism that make this novel a "lost masterpiece." The novel richly deserved its 1987 Horn Book Honor List citation and now deserves a second look as a teachable work for upper level high school students.

BIBLIOGRAPHY

Kelly, Patricia P. "Margaret (May) Mahy." 307-15 in *Writers for Young Adults*, Vol. 2, ed.Ted Hipple, Charles Scribner's Sons: New York, 1997

Mahy, Margaret. *The Catalogue of the Universe*. New York: Puffin Books, 1985.

Rincón, Carlos. "The Peripheral Center of Postmodernism: On Borges, Garcia Márquez, and Alterity," *Boundary* 2, 30, (Fall 1993): 162-79.

Patricia P. Kelly is director of the Center for Teacher Education at Virginia Tech and a professor of English education. Former co-editor of *The ALAN Review* and a past president of ALAN, she has written several book chapters and articles on young adult literature.

Chapter Twenty

Portrait of Abuse: *Cages of Glass, Flowers of Time* by Charlotte Culin

Cindy Dobrez

I am fortunate to have been a teenager in the seventies during the dawning of young adult literature. Despite having to endure the hideous combination of smock tops and low-rise elephant bell pants, my adolescence was enriched by the early novels of Judy Blume, Robert Cormier, Lois Duncan, Richard Peck, and Paul Zindel. I spent many painful teenage hours in the comfort of books. *Cages of Glass, Flowers of Time* was published in 1979, the fall I started college, so I didn't read it as a teen. Ten years later I read the book and have remained haunted by this story of child abuse, trust, ghosts, and salvation.

Before reading it myself, I heard my co-worker, Yvonne Pretzer, booktalk it many times to students in our junior high school library. They flocked to the book after hearing about Claire Burden's abandonment by her father, abuse by her mother, and her secret forbidden activity—art. Like our students, I was drawn to the book as well. However, since Yvonne focused on reading and promoting dark, realistic problem novels and mysteries, I countered with the humorous books of the eighties, funny gems by Ellen Conford, Paula Danziger, and Gordon Korman. Somehow I never got to Culin until several years later when I changed jobs. There, in a new district, I discovered battered copies of *Cages of Glass* on my library shelves. Remembering Yvonne's powerful booktalk, I knew I had to finally read this book.

After only a few pages, I was hooked. Claire's selfish artist father has neglected her, so the court has given custody to her mother. Claire must move from her deceased paternal grandmother's lovely old home with a glass greenhouse to a run-down drab tenement house. Claire soon suffers physical and mental abuse by her mother, who had learned her abusive ways from her own mother. When Claire's mother does remember to buy groceries, the bag contains mostly beer, with a small, odd assortment of food. Claire must sometimes go without food for days and then resorts to eating half a loaf of bread to fill her stomach. She eats spaghetti cold out of the can because she is too hungry to wait to heat it. Her arms have burn marks from her mother's cigarettes, and Claire tiptoes around the house like a ghost to avoid waking her mother from another drunken stupor and raising her wrath.

Claire's salvation is drawing. Having learned the art from her father, she delights in the escape it provides. Then one day she looks at her tablet and realizes she is absentmindedly sketching the shed in the yard. Claire vows, "I wouldn't draw anything ugly, ever."[1] She knows art is her only chance to find beauty in her life. There's only one problem: her mother forbids her to draw. She wants no reminders of her former husband's obsession and makes Claire promise she will not draw. That is a promise Claire can't keep. Hiding her supplies, fearful of being caught, she only draws when her mother is asleep or at work. She also heads to the woods for new scenes to draw. There she meets an older guitar-playing black man, Daniel Beasley, who, like Claire, uses his art to soothe his soul. As is common with most abused teens, Claire tries to protect her mother. Mr. Beasley tries to help, but Claire refuses to share her troubles, unable to trust. When a teacher questions her about not feeling well, Claire thinks to herself, "Don't feel sorry for me. Don't ask questions." Outwardly, however, she forces herself to reply, "I'm fine, thanks."[2]

While *Cages of Glass* was published the same year as the horrific adult saga of abuse and incest, *Flowers in the Attic*, by V.C. Andrews,[3] it was one of the first young adult novels to tackle the subject of child abuse. In fact, the *School Library Journal* review cautioned that the book was "too serious and too chilling for comfortable reading (if you can't trust your own mother) and could quite conceivably be the source of nightmares."[4] This review seems naïve today, having been followed by many fictional books of physical child abuse during the last two decades: *Good Night, Mr. Tom*[5]; *Staying Fat for Sarah Byrnes*[6]; *What Jamie Saw*[7]; *Don't You Dare Read This, Mrs. Dunphrey*[8]; *Counterfeit Son*[9]; and *You Don't Know Me*.[10] In all of these novels, at least one parent is not to be trusted. Teens in young adult literature often grapple with serious and horrific situations, as do the real teens who read these books. While the *Horn Book* review praised the "emotional immediacy," in *Cages of Glass* and the powerfully presented "bleakly realistic scenes," it also pointed out that, "The plot is full of unlikely coincidences more suitable for an old-fashioned romantic novel than for a realistic one."[11]

Admittedly, there are coincidences in this romantic tale that is also a realistic story. Clyde Bowman, a fifteen-year-old boy who grows to love Claire, befriends her despite her many attempts to push him away. In a memorable scene during a horseback ride, Clyde gently gathers Claire's long hair and ties it with a string. Claire's discomfort with this careful act shows her distrust of people and her fear of being touched. Mr. Beasley and Clyde both have ties to an earlier generation of Claire's family. Improbable, yes, but it is a small town in which they live. Any compromises in the neatly resolved plot are more than made up for in the strong development of the characters and in the richly created mood. Teens will enjoy the blossoming romance and the added mystery of a family ghost. It is Claire, though, who appears the most ghost-like throughout the novel, as she struggles to not be seen. The happy ending that finds Claire in the legal care of her art teacher, back living in her grandmother's beautiful home, is satisfying to teens who may consider this story a fairy tale of sorts. A review in the *Voice of Youth Advocates* declared this, "A beautifully written heartwarming novel . . . A well deserved nominee for the YASD Best Books list."[12]

The very publication of the book itself might be credited to a coincidence. Judy Blume met Charlotte Culin at a conference and read a few chapters of Culin's manuscript. Liking it, Blume suggested she send it to her editor, Richard Jackson. Pleased with the voice in the few pages he read, he worked with the author for three years, and when it was published, *Cages of Glass, Flowers of Time* made the final list of YASD Best Books for 1979 and was later represented with a booktalk in Joni Bodart's *Booktalk! 2*.[13] Unfortunately, *Cages of Glass* is currently out of print, with no hope of being reissued, despite recent attempts by its original editor. Charlotte Culin only published this one novel, which prevents it from getting further attention. My library paperback copy is falling apart from use, regardless of a dated, jaundiced cover that lacks current shelf appeal. The original hardcover features an appropriate oil painting portrait of Claire on the cover, but it is not attractive to teens either. It is sadly ironic that a book about art has become a lost "masterpiece." In all too many libraries the book may have been withdrawn due to lack of circulation as the result of not being promoted. In other libraries, irreplaceable copies have fallen apart from use. Current reader reviews posted at online bookstores lament its being out of print, and in response to my YALSA-BK listserv post, I received many replies from librarians and teachers who want to see it back in print. I'm almost afraid to booktalk my last copy, for fear that it will disintegrate. Yet I do promote it, and I could always use a dozen copies for my students instead of the single copy I have. As a librarian, it is maddening to have an audience for a favorite book and not be able to meet the need.

In the eighties, teens were devouring Tori Hayden's nonfiction accounts of abused children, and more recently young adults have been reading David Pelzer's personal accounts in *A Child Called "It"*[14] and its sequels. Interest among teens about child abuse accounts, factual or fiction, is high. Certainly, adult reactions and social policy related to child abuse have improved since the publication of this novel and earlier titles (*Bruises* by Anke de Vries,[15] *The Lottery Rose* by Irene Hunt,[16] and *Don't Hurt Laurie* by Willo Davis Roberts[17]), yet the basic needs of abused teens remain. The themes of trust, friendship, and hope are important for teens to consider. More importantly, these are topics that capture a teen's heart and interest. I'm sorry that I missed reading this book as a teen, but I am glad to have found it. Culin may not have been as prolific as many of my other favorite young adult authors, but she created one story that many of us will never forget.

NOTES

1. Charlotte Culin, *Cages of Glass, Flowers of Time* (Scarsdale, New York: Bradbury Press, 1979), 22.

2. Culin, *Cages*, 51.

3. V. C. Andrews, *Flowers in the Attic* (New York: Simon & Schuster, 1979).

4. Karen Ritter, review of *Cages of Glass, Flowers of Time*, *School Library Journal* 26, no. 10 (October 1979): 158.

5. Michelle Magorian, *Good Night, Mr. Tom* (New York: Harper & Row, 1981).

6. Chris Crutcher, *Staying Fat for Sarah Byrnes* (New York: Greenwillow, 1993).

7. Carolyn Coman, *What Jamie Saw* (Arden, NC: Front Street Press, 1995).

8. Margaret Peterson Haddix, *Don't You Dare Read This, Mrs. Dumphrey* (New York: Simon & Schuster Books for Young Readers, 1996).

9. Elaine Marie Alphin, *Counterfeit Son* (San Diego: Harcourt Brace, 2000).

10. David Klass, *You Don't Know Me* (New York: Frances Foster Books, 2001).

11. Paul Heins, review of *Cages of Glass, Flowers of Time*, *Horn Book Magazine* 55, no. 6 (December 1979): 668.

12. Barbara Newmark, review of *Cages of Glass, Flowers of Time*, *Voice of Youth Advocates* 2, no. 6 (February 1980): 28.

13. Joni Bodart, *Booktalk! 2: Booktalking for All Ages and Audiences* (New York: H. W. Wilson, 1985), 167-68.

14. David Pelzer, *A Child Called "It"* (Deerfield Beach, FL: Health Communications, 1995).

15. Anke de Vries, *Bruises* (Arden, NC: Front Street Press, 1995).

16. Irene Hunt, *The Lottery Rose* (New York: Scribner, 1976).

17. Willo Davis Roberts, *Don't Hurt Laurie* (New York: Atheneum, 1977).

BIBLIOGRAPHY

Carter, Frances. "Cages of Glass, Flowers of Time." 167–68 in *Booktalk! 2: Booktalking for All Ages and Audiences,* by Joni Bodart. New York: H. W. Wilson, 1985.

Culin, Charlotte. *Cages of Glass, Flowers of Time*. Scarsdale, New York: Bradbury Press, 1979. Hardcover.

———. *Cages of Glass, Flowers of Time*. New York: Dell Publishing, 1982. Paperback.

Heins, Paul. Review of *Cages of Glass, Flowers of Time*. *Horn Book Magazine*, 55, no. 6 (December 1979): 668.

Newmark, Barbara. Review of *Cages of Glass, Flowers of Time*. *Voice of Youth Advocates*, 2, no. 6 (February 1980): 28.

Ritter, Karen. Review of *Cages of Glass, Flowers of Time*. *School Library Journal*, 26, no. 10 (October, 1979): 158.

Cindy Dobrez is a middle school librarian with the West Ottawa Public School District in Holland, MI. A graduate of Indiana University's MLS program, she has published articles in many professional journals and co-authors a column for Michigan's *Media Spectrum* called "Shout it Out! The Power of PR."

Chapter Twenty One

The Quartzsite Trip by William Hogan: A Life-Changing Week
Joni Richards Bodart

It was the spring of 1962, and at John Muir High School, in Los Angeles, California, P. J. Cooper gave out invitations to the Quartzsite Trip. P. J. Cooper taught English at John Muir High and was the only person who had been on all of the Quartzsite Trips. He had been born in Quartzsite, Arizona, and had invented the trip on a whim seven years ago. (Bodart, 291)

From the first time I read this novel, the story of the irreverent, eccentric, madcap English teacher who takes thirty-six incompatible high school seniors on a week-long camping trip in the Arizona desert to discover themselves and each other, captured me, heart and mind. This work is one of the quintessential novels of adolescence, letting the reader into the minds, hearts, fears, and hopes of the teens who take the trip. They may have been born in 1945, but they deal with many of the same problems that adolescents face today. And prodding them into situations and combinations they'd never dreamed of is P. J., their teacher, whom they thought of as one of their own, the kind of teacher every teen yearns to have.

The Quartzsite Trip is set in a fictitious LA high school, during the first two weeks of April, 1962. Two epilogues reveal glimpses of the subsequent lives of some of the characters. Flashbacks reveal P. J.'s past, and a somewhat non-sequential layering of story lines and perspectives adds complexity and allows the reader to see characters from inside their own heads as well as from others' perspectives. The setting, which builds carefully with lists of what people were doing, saying, reading, watching, and buying in 1962, brings the reader into the time frame of the novel.

P. J. Cooper is the center of the book, the hub around which the members of the Quartzsite Trip circle. He sees himself as a kind of Pied Piper, and life as an adventure to be lived. He loves being a teacher, and teaches literature "as if it were a personal hobby, which it was, and not a classroom subject" (8). He delights in shaking up his students, in making them look at each other, themselves, and their ideas in new ways.

But if he likes to unsettle his students in the classroom, his ultimate attempt to give them new perspectives is the Quartzsite Trip. While his invitations to it seem random, they are not. As he tells his wife Nora, he has to make the trip because he's invited

> "a couple going steady ... one of the song girls, and the editor of the yearbook and his assistant who does all the work, and a goofy kid from the band. I've got to get them out there, all together, or it'll never happen!"
> "What will never happen?"
> "What's supposed to!" (62).

P. J. uses the Quartzsite Trip to show his students, if they choose to see it, who they are and who they might become, and in so doing changes their lives forever.

Deeter Moss, the "goofy kid from the band" (62), is the most-visible student on the trip. He steps into view on the first page and doesn't walk off stage until the last. He plays clarinet in the school band and orchestra, and "had learned to live by his wits. . . . [He] had neither the size, the strength, the coordination, the wardrobe, nor the beauty that made for popularity. . . . He did not care about status. He kept himself from being hurt" (21). This situation changes with Deeter's invitation to the Quartzsite Trip and the instant status it confers. What does not change is his own level of comfort with himself and who he is both mentally and physically. Unlike the other boys on the trip, he doesn't worry about his penis being too small, and he wears a straw cowboy hat and a red bandana that he buys at one of the stops the bus makes on the way to Quartzsite. He expects the other students to make fun of him for both these things, but he doesn't care.

Margaret Ball, studious ugly duckling, is his female counterpart, another student who sees herself clearly and dispassionately. Assistant yearbook editor, she has a futile crush on Phil Baker, the editor. She shows more sophistication in her matter of fact acceptance of her body and its functions than the popular girls who are on the trip. In several excruciatingly funny scenes, she agrees to buy sanitary napkins for Mary Allbright, who is popular, but too worried about what the boys will say about her purchase to buy them herself. Mary doesn't realize until it's far too late that Margaret has bought Tampax, which is what she has always used, instead of the Modess napkins Mary's mother buys for her.

The other students on the trip are a cagily-mixed bag of pukes, jocks, good girls, and whores, none of whom know exactly why they have been invited on the Quartzsite Trip, or exactly what the trip itself is supposed to be. In the beginning, they relate to each other as they did at school, breaking up into predictable groups. But gradually, as P. J. carefully upsets the high school hierarchy, the students realize that their previous school status or lack of it is of no value in this desert environment. For all thirty-six students, perceptions shift, opinions change, and new insight and information are revealed. It is the triumph of the underdog, told in a believable and realistic way, as the students begin to divest themselves of prior assumptions and stereotypes.

In contrast, a more serious, even sinister thread is woven through the Quartzsite Trip's adventures, as P. J., from inside his own head, dares the universe to prove it is more powerful than he is. Like the teens on the trip, P. J. has decided he is invincible, and equal to his concept of God, whom he calls the Great Equalizer. But the universe proves him wrong, and his own adolescent cockiness is his downfall, as he dies saving Deeter from a flash flood at dawn on the last day of the trip. Once again, the others' lives and perceptions shift as they come to grips with this ultimate tragedy, and the last lessons of the last Quartzsite Trip: not only are people different from whom they first appear to be, they are also not invincible, even when they believe they are. Each of us controls our world only to the extent that we control ourselves. The unexpected is always waiting for us. The Great Equalizer rules.

But what else do P. J. and his students have to say to teens today? What they've always said—people are more than they seem to be, and geeks may have talents, assets, or skills others may someday envy. All are afraid they don't look right or fit in, physically or socially, even the popular kids and the jocks. Losers can win, and winners lose. Sex is fun and scary and mysterious. Seeing situations and persons from a different perspective can change how you think and feel about them.

Hogan presents the eternal problems and fears of adolescence, and allows readers to realize that they are not alone with them. The students at John Muir High School are like teens today:

> Girls worried that their breasts weren't big enough. Boys worried that their penises were too small. They worried about zits and hard-ons and menstrual blood and bad breath. They were afraid of being laughed at, of liking the wrong thing, of saying the wrong thing at the wrong time. (31)

While this novel is set in the past, it is not historical fiction, but a timeless portrait and compelling mirror of adolescence.

Many things about teens today are strikingly different from the students on that last Quartzsite Trip, but more are just as strikingly similar. The high school hierarchy still rules, the same things still make kids either popular or not. Their feelings and fears are the same ones every new generation of teenagers has to deal with. The characters' voices are just as genuine today as they were in 1962, as are the occasionally vulgar words they use, and the adolescent society they describe. Multiple perspectives and non-sequential story lines allow the reader to see beyond the assumptions and stereotypes to the real person they hide. Like the students on the Quartzsite Trip, readers are challenged to consider who they and others are, and who they might become.

Finally, in P. J. Cooper, the reader has a portrait of a true teacher, who teases and inspires and persuades them to learn both in and out of the classroom. A teacher who gives As to the students who challenge him, and Bs to those who parrot his own words back to him. A teacher who makes his students laugh at him and at themselves, who gives them the unexpected, the unmentionable, and the unbelievable. A teacher no one ever forgets, and one who may still inspire readers to follow in his footsteps.

Although this novel is out of print, the magic and the mystery, the triumphs and the fears, the laughter and the lessons of *The Quartzsite Trip* resonate today just as they did in 1962 and 1980. "It is something that the Great Equalizer takes care of" (307).

BIBLIOGRAPHY

Bodart, Joni. *Booktalk! 2: Booktalking for All Ages and Audiences*. New York: H. W. Wilson, 1985.

Hogan, William. *The Quartsize Trip*. New York: Atheneum, 1980.

Joni Richards Bodart, a leading expert in booktalking and a school and library writer and consultant, is a faculty member in Library and Information Services at the University of Denver. Her most recent book is *Radical Reads: 101 YA Novels on the Edge* (Scarecrow Press, 2002).

Chapter Twenty Two

Her Own Way: Pragmatic Abstinence in Norma Fox Mazer's *Up in Seth's Room*

Jennifer Hubert

Since the publication of Judy Blume's *Forever* in 1975, young adult authors have continued to challenge traditional boundaries regarding teen sexuality. Early examples include Bruce and Carol Hart's 1978 sexy rock and roll romance *Sooner Later*, Sonia Levitin's 1982 take on first-time sex during senior year in *The Year of Sweet Senior Insanity*, and Nancy Garden's perennially banned classic, *Annie on My Mind*, a same-sex love story, also published in 1982. These trailblazers, along with others, fully opened the Pandora's Box of adolescent sexuality, resulting in an open and frank literary discussion of teenage love and sex the likes of which had not been seen before.

But while many of those post-*Forever* novels argued that adolescent sex is an inevitable occurrence, if not advocating it outright, there was one notable exception: *Up in Seth's Room* by Norma Fox Mazer. Published a scant four years after *Forever*, *Up in Seth's Room* was revolutionary for its time, not because the characters went all the way, but because they didn't. Fifteen-year-old protagonist Finn and her nineteen-year-old boyfriend Seth talk about intercourse, argue about intercourse, and finally end up doing something which, though not technically sex according to a former president, is fairly close to intercourse. Yet, Mazer chose to withhold that final step, a choice that was unpopular among critics still applauding Blume's brave foray into the formerly taboo topic of underage sexual relationships. One critic called Finn's reluctance to give up her maidenhead, despite her acceptance of "every other form of intimacy," a "medieval attitude."[1] Another stated that Finn's halfway approach to sex was "a ludicrous solution these days when technical virginity has pretty much lost its cachet."[2] But while critics wrangled over the supposed indecision of Finn's will-she-won't-she status, they seemingly missed Mazer's main point: Finn was an active agent of her own sexual destiny long before the term "grrrl power." Arthea J. S. Reed, agrees: "One of the things the reviewers of *Up in Seth's Room* miss in the novel is the strength of Finn. She remains true to herself."[3] Finn is a unique character in post-*Forever* young adult literature, not just because she chooses to wait for intercourse, but in the reason and manner in which she makes that choice.

At the novel's start, spirited fifteen-year-old Finn Rousseau has firmly decided that sex isn't for her, despite the fact that her best friend Vida has done the deed, and her older sister Maggie has decided to move in with her boyfriend, sans wedding rings. "Too soon. Too young. Too important" (17), she states simply when Vida presses her to at least consider sex as an option. However, when Finn meets nineteen-year-old Seth at her sister's apartment on New Year's Eve, her formerly rock solid conviction begins to waver. Seth is, in today's teen slang, a "total hottie." For Finn, it is practically love at first sight. As the unlikely romance between Finn, the conscientious student and devoted daughter, and Seth, the rebellious high school drop-out, begins to blossom, Finn finds herself battling both her hormones and her conscience as she and Seth grow increasingly intimate. They have been naked together in the bed of Seth's rented room, exploring bodies and feelings. She knows she's not ready for intercourse, but she longs for the closeness and sharing that physical intimacy brings. What to do?

Norma Fox Mazer sets up a stereotypical situation with Finn stuck between two extremes: to go all the way, or batten down the hatches and be labeled a prude. But Mazer blasts through the stereotype by giving Finn the tools to get herself out of this mess; namely, a brain and some common sense. Finn is no fool. Through her characterization of Finn as a stalwart young woman who refuses to be swayed by society or peers, Mazer demonstrates she is a writer who both acknowledges and admires the intelligence and strength of which teenagers are capable. And being just such a teen, Finn creates her own third option—pragmatic abstinence. For Finn, pragmatic abstinence means coming up with a definition of sex that works for her, and then sticking to that definition. In an article responding to some of the criticism of *Seth's Room*, Norma Fox Mazer wrote,

> The young are full of passion for a sexual life; but does that have to mean "doing it"? Don't we use the word *sex* in too narrow a way? As if sex is

simply a quicker way of saying that cumbersome word *intercourse*? But of course there's a great deal more to sex than this. This is something young people need to know." (4)

As an agent of her own sexual destiny, Finn doesn't accept the commonly held definition of sex as intercourse, her first step towards pragmatic abstinence.

But when it comes to standing by her personal definition of sex, Finn has a harder time convincing Seth to join her. He gives her a laundry list of sexual myths that teens both then and now have heard so often that they have come to accept them as true, such as "Girls always say no at first" (119), "Lots of people are scared the first time"(169), and, perhaps worst of all, "everyone knows you have to convince some girls"(182). But Finn isn't just "some girl." She counters with "The way I heard it, both people were supposed to want to"(170) and when Seth demands she tell him she's his and his alone, Finn emphatically states, "I'm Finn's"(154). But lest the reader wonder if Finn is perfect in her pragmatism, Mazer builds in some self-doubt, a trait any teenager can understand. "Had she been wrong to say no? What if she'd just let it happen? It would have made Seth happy. And her? He thought it would make her happy, too. . . .What if she *was* wrong? Why not? What made *her* infallible? What made her know so positively"(173)?

Happily, Finn's method of pragmatic abstinence ends up working for her and maybe unsurprisingly, Seth. After they break up because of their continual arguments about sex, Seth runs into her again at her sister's apartment, when they have both had time to think: ". . . why did I start pressing you? The only thing I can figure out is that somehow I've gotten the idea that sleeping with a girl is the *only* thing that counts"(190). Once Seth accepts that making out isn't just a means to an end, he and Finn are able to move together towards an intimacy that is mutually acceptable to them both. In taking control of her own destiny and not giving into societal or peer pressure, Finn hasn't only helped herself, but Seth as well. Seth has matured as a person because Finn has taught him that all the stereotypical axioms he held about women and sex were pure myth. Although at the end of the novel Seth leaves to pursue a job in another state, he and Finn part as friends, each of them having learned a valuable lesson about sex and love.

Is *Up in Seth's Room* a young adult masterwork worthy of republication? Considering when and why Mazer wrote it, yes. To admit that teens have sexual desire and that they can do something about it besides take cold showers or give into it completely is a realistic and practical solution to the age-old problem of raging adolescent hormones. Mazer's point that teens can take responsibility for their desire, and become active agents of their own sexual destinies is powerful and appropriate for a modern youth population that is often portrayed as mindless, sex-driven consumers who exist only to buy name brand sneakers and concert tickets. Mazer tells us the opposite—that there are many teens like Finn, individuals strong enough to listen to their consciences rather than heed the pervasive purr of material and societal pressures. Once teens see that third option of pragmatic abstinence validated, they could begin to realize that sexual destiny is only one of the many destinies in their lives that they are capable of controlling. Norma Fox Mazer expertly took a loaded topic and used it to show that teenagers, so often maligned as thoughtless and silly, can actually analyze the consequences of life-altering choices and, more often than not, make the right decision. As appropriate and necessary now as the day it was published, *Up in Seth's Room* is the stuff of which YA masterworks are made.

NOTES

1. Campbell, Patty. *Wilson Library Bulletin* (October 1979): 123, 139.
2. *Kirkus* Review (December 1979): 1380.
3. Arthea J. S. Reed, *Norma Fox Mazer: A Writer's World* (Lanham, MD: Scarecrow Press, 2000), 45.
4. Norma Fox Mazer, "Up in Seth's Room: Some Thoughts," *The ALAN Review* (Fall 1980): 1.

BIBLIOGRAPHY

Mazer, Norma Fox. *Up in Seth's Room.* New York: Delacorte, 1979.
———. "Up in Seth's Room: Some Thoughts." *The ALAN Review* (Fall 1980): 1.
Reed, Arthea J.S. *Norma Fox Mazer: A Writer's World.* Lanham, Md: Scarecrow Press, 2000.

Jennifer Hubert is the middle school/coordinating librarian at the Little Red School House & Elisabeth Irwin High School in Manhattan. She is also the author of *Reading Rants! Out of the Ordinary Teen Booklists* (http://tln.lib.mi.us/~amutch/jen) and a regular reviewer of young adult books for *Amazon.com*.

Chapter Twenty Three

"We Cut Ourselves": Revisiting *Crosses* by Shelley Stoehr
Patrick Jones

With a first line of "We cut ourselves," *Crosses* by Shelly Stoehr starts with a loud smack and never lets up. *Crosses* tells the story of Katie and Nancy, two Long Island high school students, who cut their own skin with sharp objects. But cutting is only one of many self-injurious behaviors the book examines. Nancy abuses drugs and alcohol (an abuse her parents share); she is abused verbally by her parents, socially by her classmates, physically by her boyfriend, and raped by an acquaintance. Katie shares a similar catalog of agony and addictions. *Crosses* isn't loaded with artistic images painting a pretty picture of teen lives, but instead is a gritty, slightly out-of-focus snapshot of a teenage wasteland.

At the center of this wasteland is high school. The action isn't in the classrooms, but in the bathrooms where Katie and Nancy steal away to smoke, drink, and cut. Nancy has always "fit in" and is expected by her parents to fit in with all the normal kids at school. She is an outcast by choice, fighting off her previous "good girl" image. She dives heavily into the party scene with its drinking, drugging, and sexual activity. These scenes portray teens in a manner that is not nice, maybe not even normal for all teens, but certainly a reality for some young people, in particular those who have become disconnected from their surroundings as Nancy and Katie have.

Crosses is not a problem novel; it is a pain novel. The book is about a totally new problem. No young adult novel before *Crosses* had ever dealt with cutting or punk characters like Katie and Nancy, and few dealt with the darker sides of teen life in this honest fashion until *Crosses* emerged in 1991. Almost every scene seems to take place in a cloud of cigarette or marijuana smoke, a haze of alcohol or drugs, and with loud music crashing around the characters. Nancy and Katie's lives are a catalog of risk-taking behavior. They "know" better; they are both smart, but they are convinced they won't get caught, and are not overly concerned with any possible consequences. They live up to their motto "What is life without risk?" Like all teens, Nancy and Katie are making a series of choices, but without the strong anchor of family, friends, community, or school, the choices are the easy ones, the self-destructive ones. Other than each other, they have only a few other friends. They have lots of free time, access to money to buy drugs, and people in their lives who "enable" them.

The risky behavior is made even riskier by Nancy's lack of concern. Occasionally she is disgusted with her actions, but those bouts of introspection are few and far between. Her lack of acceptance is coupled with her boredom. Without a lot of other friends, with no home life, and with considerable intelligence that lets her get by with little time or effort spent on homework, Nancy talks often about being bored. The drugs and the cutting are the kicks she needs to feel something. *Crosses* isn't meant as a nice read; it is a wild rant by a young woman in a great deal of pain; because she doesn't feel accepted at home, at school, or anywhere in the world, she must manifest the agony of alienation through self-mutilation.

Nancy's voice is strong, real, and angry. Her vocabulary, and that of the other characters, is filled with curse words and slang. They don't feel bad, they feel shitty. Things are not rotten, they suck. Nancy uses the word "fuck" often, creatively, and in all variations. "Fuck you" is Nancy and Katie's all-purpose expression to someone they feel has hurt them. Many of the conversations in *Crosses* are not dialogues, they are shouting matches. The book is filled with conflict: the short violent stabs Nancy makes in her skin mirror the short violent stabs that pass for communication.

The book moves quickly. Months click off; each chapter announces the time of year or how much time has passed since the previous chapter. The pacing is rapid; the book takes the characters from scene to scene at a breakneck speed. They never seem to relax; the intensity of the prose mirrors the insanity and intensity of their lives. The pace of the book, the harshness of the language, and the dialogue—more often screamed rather than spoken—is like the punk music that Nancy and Katie listen, relate, and dress to. Like *Go Ask Alice,* to which *Crosses* is often compared, the soundtrack of the book mirrors not only the times, but the lives of the characters. They are involved physically in things they cannot handle emotionally. The chasm between the two becomes a spiraling abyss into which Nancy and Katie fall.

Stoehr's first book did not go unnoticed, in part because of the widespread discussion among critics, teachers, and librarians that the book was "harmful" to teens. The book wasn't harmful, it was simply ahead of its time. In so many ways, *Crosses* was a trailblazer for later, more literary books, such as Laurie Halse Anderson's *Speak*. The matter-of-fact grimness of *The Facts Speak for Themselves* by Brock Cole or the grittiness of so many late 1990s young adult novels owe a debt to Stoehr's debut book. The drug use in a book like *Smack* by Melvin Burgess, the sexuality in novels like James Bennett's *Plunking Reggie Jackson*, or the general sense of hard times in Sarah Dessen's *Dreamland* echo back to *Crosses*. While it did win a few honors, including an honor award in the Delacorte Press Prize for Best First Young Adult Novel, *Crosses* is not much recalled or respected, failing to make YALSA's best of the best or other such lists.

This neglect stems, perhaps, from three primary factors. While Stoehr's follow-up effort, *Weird on the Outside*, received some positive reviews, the same cannot be said for her two following books: *Wannabe* and *Forever Wendy*. Neither landed on a best list, and *Forever Wendy* was almost universally panned. While Stoehr has bounced back with a few published short stories, it has been almost four years since her last novel. Her inability to continue to publish respected fiction certainly harms the reputation of even a book as fine as *Crosses*. The second problem is the book's Hollywood ending. After playing hardball for most of the novel, the finale featuring the quick accidental death of Katie coupled with the miracle salvation/family reunification of Nancy reduces what could have been a recognized classic into merely a good book. Third, and perhaps most important is that while *Crosses* was "cutting edge" at the time of its publication, it now pales in comparison to works of later authors whose grit was truer and whose vision is broader. The cutting edge that was *Crosses* has become the status quo as everything moves toward the center.

Crosses is not so much a coming-of-age story as a tale of survival in a teenage wasteland of disconnected parents. This negative portrayal of parents makes many teachers, librarians, and reviewers (often parents themselves) very nervous. The carnage of Nancy and Katie's life is going on right under the noses of various adults. Their teachers and school counselors are either portrayed as ineffectual or too trusting. Katie's parents barely appear. Her father was last seen two years ago, while the mother, who works as a teacher, merely comes home long enough to change clothes and then go out trolling for men. Nancy's parents are her main antagonists, in particular her mother. It is not pretty. There are few conversations, mostly shouting matches. They talk at a high volume, but they don't hear each other. Not surprisingly, the only way Nancy's mother can make a point is to strike her. Nancy is the product of a classically dysfunctional household ruled by fear, soaked with alcohol, in which problems are solved with brutality.

Yet perhaps *Crosses'* legacy as a lost masterwork of young adult fiction is the way Stoehr takes almost every YA convention and turns it around. Characters in most YA books follow a pattern: they have a problem, and then throughout the book, they work toward solving it. *Crosses* is the exact opposite: the characters have many problems and rather than solving them, they only seem to make them worse. They are searching for their next high, the next shock, not a solution. They see around them, in the other kids at schools, in their parents, but mostly in the suburban world they inhabit, nothing but hostility. They react by drawing closer to each other; drawing crosses in their skin, and drawing marijuana and other drugs into their system. Perhaps *Crosses* is not so much a lost book as one that is avoided because it hits so hard in describing Nancy and Katie's walk through their teenage wasteland.

BIBLIOGRAPHY

Lesesne, Teri S. "Forget-Me-Nots: Books Worth a Second Look." *The ALAN Review* 25, no.2 (Winter 1998): 52-54.

Mitchell, Diana and Pat Zipper. "Children of Alcoholics in Shelley Stoehr's *Crosses:* Teens + Alcoholic Parents = Problems." In *Using Literature to Help Troubled Teenagers Cope with Family Issues,* ed. Joan F. Kaywell. Westport, CT: Greenwood Press. 1999.

Stoehr, Shelley. "Controversial Issues in the Lives of Contemporary Young Adults." *The ALAN Review* 24, no. 2 (Winter 1997), 3-5.

Patrick Jones runs Connectingya.com, a consulting firm dedicated to providing library youth services. He has published three books: *Running a Library Card Campaign*, *Connecting Young Adults and Libraries*, and *Do It Right: Customer Service for Young Adults in School and Public Libraries*. He is the author of the first volume in the Scarecrow Press Young Adult Series, *What's So Scary About R. L. Stine?* He recently completed his first YA novel, *Things Change*.

Chapter Twenty Four

Blinded by the Light by Robin Brancato: A Forgotten Masterwork
Robert C. Small

I remember vividly when I first encountered Robin Brancato's *Blinded by the Light*. It was published in 1978, and the author was scheduled to be a speaker at the 1979 National Council of Teachers of English Fall Conference. I had a copy of the book but had not yet read it. I was looking forward to hearing her speak and brought the book to the conference with me. That late fall was the same time when the Jonestown massacre took place in northwest Guyana in South America. Each day as conference attendees met in San Francisco, the newspapers were filled with the horrible events as over nine hundred of the approximately eleven hundred followers of Jim Jones, the master of the cult known as "The People's Temple," were discovered to have killed themselves or were murdered by being forced to drink Kool-Aid mixed with cyanide. It was in that almost unreal milieu that I sat down and read *Blinded by the Light*.

Brancato did deliver her speech. In it she told us that she had been interested in cults for many years. She remembered meeting with some of the followers of a famous cult leader of that time, Father Divine. She returned to the subject of cults after reading numerous stories about their growing popularity in the years leading up to the writing of the book. She described her research to prepare for writing the book, including having herself invited to participate in a three-day weekend information meeting of a then popular cult, the Unification Church of Sun Myung Moon. She shared with us the feelings of unease and sense of being drawn in against her will and the fact that she escaped as she described it, after the second day, as does Gail, the novel's protagonist, in her first encounter with a religious cult. Reading the novel and then listening to

Brancato tell the story of her involvement with the cult as more horrors of Jonesboro were being discovered was truly unforgettable.

Blinded by the Light tells the story of Gail Brower, a sophomore in college, whose brother Jim has joined the religious cult, Light of the World (LOW), shortly before he was to graduate from the same college where Gail is a student. She and her parents are alarmed and anxious, and each sets out to try to find and rescue him. Gail's roommate, Marilyn, and her lover, Doug, question whether Gail should interfere with Jim's right to make his own decisions. Gail rejects their concerns. She believes that, if she can talk with him, she can convince him to leave the cult, and so she lets herself be invited to a retreat held by LOW for prospective members. At the retreat, she discovers that Jim will be in Philadelphia in a few days for a rally of the organization where its leader, Father Adam, will speak. But she also discovers that the techniques that the cult members use to draw in new members are effective even when used on someone such as herself who knows who they are and what they are trying to do. These techniques are shown as nearly constant flattery and affection to make her feel she is a loved member of the group already, constant talk about the wonders of the cult's beliefs and its leader, and so much constant activity that she is exhausted much of the time. The cult also appeals to potential new members' urges to be free of the need to make decisions.

The novel presents an insightful look at the relative ease with which many young people can be drawn into going along with a group, although one review called this insight "a highly questionable assumption, and a message of dubious value to adolescents" (Fisher, 17), a comment that seems hopelessly out of touch with the reality then and certainly the reality of schools today with their cliques, gangs, and bullied outsiders. As Charlie, a cult recruiter says, "Gail, come with us please. Whatever you're looking for, we can help you find it. We can help you turn your life around. Will you?" (29). Later in the novel, in a vivid depiction of this state, Brancato writes," Gail looked again at Jim's upturned face. His eyes were shining, his hands clasped in ecstasy. She watched the other faces. Radiant, flushed. Like Jim's. It must be nice to feel so strongly, so certainly, about something" (129).

At this point, the reader has met most of the major players in the novel: Gail; Doug; Gail and Jim's parents; Matt, the deprogrammer; and several members of the LOW. Although one critic commented, "Characterizations are two-dimensional, merely acting out their roles in the story, and Brancato oversimplifies the cult experience" (*Booklist*, 175), the characterization is effective in creating not only representations of the types of individuals that would be involved in such a situation but also, in most cases, individuals whose personalities and emotions are vivid and living for the reader. An exception is the characterization of most of the members of the cult. They are largely one-dimensional and alike in their surface presentation as positive, loving individuals wholly devoted to Father Adam and the cult. This way of dealing with these characters, however, certainly fits the image both of the cult members as people and as recruiters of new members.

Finally, Gail does meet with Jim and tries to persuade him to come home. She, however, is persuaded by him to stay for the rally when he agrees to come home for a day. Gradually, she finds herself being drawn into the cult by the very techniques she had detected earlier. One critic rejected this insight, stating, "Brancato's contention that just 24 hours of little sleep and less food could turn someone as level-headed as Gail into a mind-blown zombie . . . is hard to swallow" (*Kirkus*, 1191-92). Yet in the context of the novel, and, given what we know about the effects of various chemicals on our moods, it is certainly believable.

After a weak effort to resist, "She closed her eyes and let herself be carried along with the crowd" (134). However, Doug, is there:

> Suddenly she felt a hand grip hers, tug it hard. She resisted involuntarily and then whirled around, dropping her bag and clapping her hand to her mouth.
>
> "Don't talk," Doug warned, in a single motion picking up her bag and yanking her through the empty row in the opposite direction from the way she'd been going. "Put your head down. Move fast," he whispered, as he bucked the pile-up of people and pulled her through the exit at the base of the steps and into the dark hall. (134–35)

After the attempt at a forced rescue by her parents and a hired deprogrammer failed with Jim, Gail does have one last chance to talk with him. Although he knows the techniques used to draw him into the cult: "'I admitted there are things that are hard to accept. But *I've accepted them*, Gail!' he said, smiling calmly. 'I have to, once I accept Father Adam. All those things are unimportant, means to an end, and the end is the world of love with Father at the helm'" (164). The meeting ends with Jim agreeing to meet with Gail and Doug in order to live up to his earlier promise. Though the meeting seems assured, the last words of the novel suggest a doubt: "'See you Sunday,' she said. And then, impressing in her memory the way he looked, she squeezed his hand hard before she turned away and let go" (166). This ambiguous ending gives real strength to the situation in which Gail, Jim, and other cult members find themselves. As one critic pointed out, "No final conclusion is reached but the no-man's land of decision making is painted in somber tones, clearly underlining the fact that few situations are all black or all white" (Gray, 406).

Despite some mixed initial reviews, *Blinded by the Light* was excerpted in *Scholastic Magazine* in February 1979, and the Bantam edition appeared in May of 1979, both prior to the attention given to cults because of the Jonestown massacre. Also, the Columbia Broadcasting System made the novel into a "Movie of the Week," the first showing of which was in December 1980. Unfortunately, the novel is no longer available and rarely appears in lists of recommended reading for young readers. The insights into the power of cults as well as their approach to recruitment should, however, certainly appeal to today's young readers. Although cults are not in the headlines as much as they were at the time of the publication of *Blinded by the Light*, recent events in schools have brought to our attention the problems created by cliques and gangs and the almost desperate need that many teenagers have to find a group to belong to. Readers vicariously experience what Gail lives through as they are captured by this story of the immersion of Gail and Jim in the cult and as they see the clear way the two are manipulated.

BIBLIOGRAPHY

Brancato, Robin F. *Blinded by the Light*. New York, N.Y.:Alfred A. Knopf, 1978.

"Brancato, Robin F. 1936–." *Something about the Author*, vol 97, Detroit, MI: Gale Research, 1998, 22–27.

Davis, James. "Robin F. Brancato." 143-52 in *Writers for Young Adults*, ed. Ted Hipple. New York, NY: Charles Scribner's Sons, 1997.

DeSalvo, Louise A. "The Uses of Adversity: Robin Brancato's Novels as Patterns for Adolescent Coping." *Media and Methods*, vol. 15 (April 1979): 16, 18, 50–51.

Edwards, Edna Earl. ABrancato, Robin F(idler)." 74–75 in *Twentieth Century Young Adult Writers*, ed. Laura Stadley Berger. Detroit, MI: St. James Press, 1994.

Fisher, Maxine. Review of *Blinded by the Light. Interracial Books for Children Bulletin*, vol. 10, no. 4 (1979): 17.

Gray, Hildagarde. Review of *Blinded by the Light. Best Sellers*, vol. 38. no. 12 (March, 1979): 406–7.

"Review of *Blinded by the Light.*" *Booklist*, vol.75, no. 2, (September 15, 1978): 175.

"Review of *Blinded by the Light.*" *Children's Literature Review*, vol 32, Detroit, MI: Gale Research, 1994, 64-75.

"Review of *Blinded by the Light.*" *Contemporary Literary Criticism*, vol. 35. Detroit, MI: Gale Research, 1985, 65–70.

"Review of *Blinded by the Light.*" *Kirkus Reviews*, vol. XLVI, no. 21 (November 1, 1978): 1191–92.

Prescott, Peter. Review of *Blinded by the Light. Newsweek*, December 18, 1978, 102.

Wooldridge, C. Nordheim. Review of *Blinded by the Light. School Library Journal,* vol. 25, no. 2 (October 1978): 152.

Robert Small is currently a member of the education faculty at Radford University. A former secondary school English teacher, he has served as NCTE's Chair of the Conference on English Education, as president of ALAN, and as co-editor of *The ALAN Review* and the 1999 publication *Two Decades of The ALAN Review.*

Chapter Twenty Five

Searching for Identity and Reconciliation: *In Summer Light* by Zibby Oneal

Patricia L. Daniel and Joan F. Kaywell

Published in 1985, *In Summer Light* received critical acclaim as an ALA Best Book for Young Adults, ALA Notable Book, School Library Journal Best Book, and Horn Book Honor selection. Today, however, it is difficult to find a copy—a used one at that—as the novel is no longer in print. It is hard to understand why, and we can only hope for a resurgence of interest.

Zibby Oneal's book depicts the emotional struggle between a father and daughter who are so much alike they crowd, and maybe even threaten, each other. Before she can appreciate and celebrate their similarities, seventeen-year-old Kate Brewer must discover who she is apart from her father. One of the merits of this book is that it gives adolescents the opportunity to see themselves in literature at a time when growing up and establishing one's identity separate from one's parents is a struggle, and always an individual journey.

The literary fabric of *In Summer Light* is expertly woven. The characters, particularly Kate, her father, and her mother, are rich and believable, and readers know their weaknesses as well as their strengths. The major conflicts, however, are between Kate and herself and between Kate and her famous artist father. The story's setting, an island on Martha's Vineyard off the coast of Massachusetts, provides a place for Kate to deal with these conflicts. Oneal confided in an interview that she considers it part of her "responsibility to make children understand that adolescence is a self-absorbed world—this may be why I always have islands in my books—but it's not a place where you can stay forever" (Smith, 98). Both literally and figuratively, Kate cannot run away from what's bothering her. The book's themes give readers much to think about and discuss: one must respect oneself and others before one can truly be independent; and independence is an awareness of one's dependence and interdependence upon others.

In her novels Oneal writes what she knows, bringing in settings and circumstances from her own life. She credits her mother, a marvelous storyteller, for introducing her to characters in stories and classics and giving her a genuine love of literature; she also credits her father, an amateur painter, for introducing her to art (Bloom, 1997). Similarly, Kate delves into both the literary and artistic worlds as she discovers, and eventually embraces, who she is and who she is becoming. As an additional artistic bonus, Oneal provides readers with wonderful images of color, permeating and enhancing the story with subtle hues and brilliant shades of paint.

As the story unfolds, Kate is forced to leave school and return to her home on the island to recuperate from mononucleosis. While there, Kate's only task for the summer is to finish an English paper on Shakespeare's *The Tempest*. Besides being prone to naps, lacking energy, being idle, and having writer's block, Kate is bothered by something else. She resents how much her mother does to please her father, and she resents her famous painter father for expecting to be adored. During her recuperation, she remembers how much, when she was younger, she had worshiped her father and imitated his painting. In fact, she considered herself an artist until her father belittled her award-winning painting with the comment, "It's a nice little picture" (68). There was a time when Kate wanted to make her father proud by painting so well that when anyone mentioned a Brewer picture, the reference would be to one of her pieces rather than her father's. After her father's devastating comment, however, she became repulsed by the smell of paints and put away her canvases and brushes altogether.

Kate explains to Leah, her school roommate, who visits one weekend, that her father needs to be the center of attention. Kate's attempt to improve as a painter in an effort to please him was counterproductive; she stopped painting rather than continuing to try. Kate does not realize that she is not responsible for her father's behavior and that she does not have to allow him control over her or her interests.

Oneal uses *The Tempest* as Kate's vehicle for seeing her father in a different light and for discovering a way to deal with her feelings of estrangement from him. Kate muses about the paper she must write, but she struggles with Shakespeare's play because of her aggravation with Prospero's character. She realizes that Prospero reminds her of her father, and she resents how everyone has made allowances for him because of his artistic genius. Kate does not realize that she must see her father as a person, apart from being her father, if she ever expects for him to be able to see *her* as a person, apart from being his daughter.

With the help of Ian, a graduate student who is cataloging her father's paintings, Kate begins to understand that she's having more than a writer's block. She realizes that she has a block centered on her relationship—or lack of one—with her egotistical father. She talks to Ian, and he helps her explore her inner self to find out why. Ian guides Kate to accept herself, including the artist she is irrespective of her artist father. Gradually, Kate realizes that she needs to overcome the bitterness she feels toward her father and that she doesn't need to disappear into the background of her father's "genius" as her mother has. Kate rediscovers her joy of painting and the energy that painting provides her.

As she begins painting again, she begins to be less self-absorbed. She volunteers to paint a portrait of Frances, the housekeeper's bratty little girl. This act is monumental because Kate has been consistently honest about her ill feelings toward Frances. By reaching beyond herself and including others—even flawed individuals in her world—Kate is able to finish her paper on Prospero and *The Tempest*. Using her insights into how her father is like Prospero and seeing how his moods and needs limit the fulfillment of those around him, Kate writes, "It is wrong, morally, politically, humanly wrong for a ruler to ignore the needs of his people. To use others for his own purposes with no concern for the cost to them is unforgivable. Prospero is guilty of these things" (146).

This realization and indictment seems to free her from the burden of her father. Instead of quietly delivering his coffee and only observing his attempt to fix the static state of his painting, Kate uncharacteristically voices her opinion about his piece. This act of speaking her mind and treading on his territory opens a long closed dialogue between the two of them. He confides that he does not have many ideas anymore, and it frightens him. He tells her his interpretation of the upcoming Retrospective Exhibit at Berkeley: "most painters aren't offered retrospective exhibits until everyone assumes that their best work is behind them" (145). This raw honesty allows Kate to see her father as an old man, and she is able to make her peace. She is stunned to see him as a person living in the past tense. She returns to her essay and adds these words:

> And yet at the end of the play, Prospero has become an old man. His magic powers are nearly gone, and then they are gone entirely. In the Epilogue he asks us to set him free. I think Shakespeare means for us to forgive him. I think he means that if we refuse, we will be trapped like Prospero was, on his island. (146)

As Oneal commented in an interview, she values the safety of the island but understands that our stay on the island must be temporary. "The movement away and out into the world, into concern for other people, has to happen; you aren't adult until you make that move. Sure, explore your feelings . . . but then get into the world" (Smith, 98). Kate has demonstrated her concern for other people in painting the portrait of Frances, and does so again toward the end of the novel when she, offended by the rudeness of a condescending professor, participates in a discussion with her father and the professor—a conversation she would have previously ignored. By participating, she acknowledges her father's life work, and, at the same time, her father agrees with her assessment of art. Finally, they are on the same side; yet, both are distinct individuals.

As readers, we can identify with Oneal's characters because each of us has to deal with growing up, becoming independent, and learning life's lessons. One of our students wrote,

> I loved her characters. Everyone she wrote about was so real to me—possibly because they reminded me of myself when I was their ages. She created introspective, artistic girls who were strong in their own ways. But then Oneal wasn't afraid to paint in their flaws and let them come undone.

As Susan Bloom (1997) aptly put it in a biography of the author, "Readers recognize themselves in . . . Kate and can transfer that sense of 'always becoming,' of never fully resolving the fundamental questions about family and self, to their own lives" (440). Finally, the reconciliation between father and daughter that occurs because of Kate's literary insight from *The Tempest* might prompt some readers to have their own literary insight from *In Summer's Light*. In that way, Kate and Oneal have certainly created their individual masterpieces.

BIBLIOGRAPHY

Bloom, Susan P., and Cathryn M. Mercer. *Presenting Zibby Oneal.* Boston: Twayne, 1991.
———. "Zibby Oneal." 433-42 in *Writers for Young Adults*, ed. Ted Hipple. New York: Charles Scribner's Sons. 1997.
Oneal, Zibby. *In Summer Light.* New York: Viking, 1985.
———. *A Formal Feeling.* New York: Viking, 1982.
———. *The Language of the Goldfish.* New York: Viking, 1980.
Shakespeare, William. "The Tempest." 1537-68 in *The Complete Signet Classic Shakespeare*, ed. Robert Langbaum. New York: Harcourt Brace Jovanovich, 1972.
Smith, Wendy. " Working Together." *Publishers Weekly* 21 (February 21, 1986): 97-98.

Patricia L. Daniel is associate professor of English education at the University of South Florida where she is director of the Tampa Bay Area Writing Project. She is published in *English Journal, Language Arts, The ALAN Review, Adolescent Literature as a Complement to the Classics, Volumes 2, 3, and 4*.

Joan F. Kaywell is professor of English education at the University of South Florida where she teaches undergraduate and graduate courses in English methods and adolescent literature. She is dedicated to promoting teen literacy and is best known for the books she has edited: *Adolescent Literature as a Complement to the Classics, Volumes 1, 2, 3,* and *4* (Christopher-Gordon) and the *Using Literature to Help Troubled Teenagers* Series (Greenwood).

Chapter Twenty Six

Some Thoughts on My First Novel Going out of Print
Marie G. Lee

I realized I wanted to be a writer the day I inherited my brother's old typewriter. I was nine. When I put in a sheet of paper, I fell in love with the way my words came out looking "professional." I typed a story, tied it with yarn, and sold it to my parents for a nickel—my first publication.

In retrospect, becoming a writer was almost inevitable. A shy child, I was an inveterate reader, much preferring an afternoon sailing the South Seas with Pippi Longstocking than trying to navigate the shoals of the elementary school social scene. I was a dud at parties; my best friend and I spent most of our time silently, our noses buried in our respective books. Judy read nonfiction; I liked stories, especially those with a surprise ending (O. Henry was to become a favorite). My new machine was all the motivation I needed to start turning out my own.

By sixth grade, my goal was to become the nation's youngest author. I finished a mystery novel that clocked in at an astounding one hundred twenty-three pages (with a properly O. Henry-ish twist at the end). I sent the manuscript to all the famous publishers, only to be crushed by reading in *Dynamite* magazine that Ally Sheedy, who wrote a book called *She Was Nice to Mice*, had trumped me by being, at eleven, the youngest published author. Washed up at twelve, I did find some solace in the encouraging rejection letters I received (and, in a further twist, Ally Sheedy's mother became my literary agent some twenty-five years later).

I still had faith. My file cabinet bulged with stories, which seemed to flow out of me as naturally as air. As a junior in high school, I wrote an essay on being in the Miss Teen Minnesota pageant (an experience too strange for fiction), and *Seventeen* published it.

In college, I began *Finding My Voice*, a YA novel loosely based on my experiences growing up Korean American on the Iron Range in Minnesota. For five years I worked on that book, sometimes rising at four in the morning to write for a few hours before leaving for my job on Wall Street.

The biggest leap of faith taken for my writing was to quit my safe, secure job to write full time, with little to recommend me except a small grant I'd won from the Society of Children's Book Writers.

The next two years were blissful because I was writing, but also fraught with anxiety because *Finding My Voice* didn't find a publisher. A few editors had kind words, nothing more. A wonderful young adult author helped me find an agent; but after a year, the agent began to believe the book was unsellable—then, at the last minute, Houghton Mifflin offered to buy both my first and second book, *If It Hadn't Been For Yoon Jun*, which had been written while waiting for FMV to sell.

Any author will tell you that the publication of the first book is unforgettable: Seeing sketches of the cover, the prepublication galleys, then finally holding the real book. I recall squinting at a smudgy fax from my editor, a paragraph of text with a *star next to my book from something called *Kirkus*. A few months later I was notified that I'd won the Friends of American Writers award, and Houghton Mifflin flew me to Chicago for the ceremony. Even more wonderful was the mail from readers; what an unexpected gift this novel, which allowed me, a bookish introvert, to make enduring connections with so many like-minded people—some of who have become friends.

I felt assured of *Finding My Voice*'s future. It was on recommended reading lists, and had even been picked up in a number of Asian American literature courses at universities such as Berkeley and UCLA. My fan mail came in from all over the country.

However, in 1988, I was working at a culture camp for Korean adoptees, and the camp director told me she couldn't get copies of FMV for the camp's book sale. Just a few days before, I remembered, a friend had mentioned she, too, was having trouble ordering it. I assured them that the book was just going through another printing, because on *Amazon.com*, it said, "temporarily out of stock."

Over the next few months, I received similar troubling complaints. But I was certain my publisher would let me know if it was considering putting the book out of print; an anthology I had contributed to had recently gone out of print, and the publisher, Avon, let me know it was happening, sent me a complimentary box of books, and offered to let me buy more at a by-the-pound price.

Eventually, I needed more copies of FMV for myself. My local bookstore said its distributor was out, so I called the publisher directly. I was told, bluntly, that the book was out of print and had been for months. No notice, no nothing, and the copies in the warehouse had long ago been pulped.

Even as a writer, I can't put into words the devastation I felt. I didn't understand—there seemed to be plenty of people who still wanted the book. A friend in publishing did some behind-the-scenes sleuthing and found that the book had indeed been let go, not as a result of a change in its sales profile, but simply because the publisher had been acquired—it was a normal practice to cut lists, the way employees are laid off after a merger.

Readers actually offered to write to my publisher to ask for reconsideration. Maybe twenty people wrote heartfelt letters. My Asian American literature colleagues circulated petitions among their students that grew to hundreds of names. The publisher didn't reply to any of them.

On my end, I was urging my agent to find another publisher. But I soon found that an out-of-print book acquires a stigma of failure. My editor at my current house rejected it, which hurt a lot. My agent said since this editor didn't even want it, there would be little hope at other publishers.

I then took it upon myself to write to editors, concentrating mostly on small, quirky publishers, and even extremely unlikely venues for YA fiction such as university presses. I was feeling a little like a used-car salesman, although instead of saying "low mileage," a "beaut," I was flinging around terms like "ALA Best Book for Reluctant Readers," "IRA Young Adults' Choice," "reviewed in the *New York Times*," but the response was always the same: must be a lemon if it went out of print.

I even began looking into self-publishing. But it was with an ever-encroaching sense of dismay that I watched the number of hours—precious writing hours—being sucked into what looked like a futile venture.

I was unexpectedly saved by the completion of my first adult novel, *Somebody's Daughter*; I felt I needed a different agent for this new phase in my career, and I was delighted when my old *She Was Nice to Mice* rival's mother took me on. Charlotte also read *Finding My Voice*, proclaimed it wonderful, and promptly sold it to HarperCollins, which, by then, had acquired my current publisher, so the poor book had traveled far and wide but had come back full circle (in yet another O. Henryish twist, the book fell into the hands of the first editor who had rejected it).

The path is not all rosy, however. The book is still used goods, and it's been delayed for years. It makes me wonder how many other beloved books have had their fates determined not by someone who's read it and knows it, but an accountant holding an ax of pure numbers. I'm not suggesting books should never go out of print, or that publishers should publish at a loss, but my fear as an author and reader is of corporate pressures causing the premature death of wonderful books. I can still remember the eye-opening and unexpected experiences I had reading a book that I found in a bookstore or library by running my fingers down spines until a title, or even a shape or cover intrigued me. Removing books from the world before their time also removes all this potential.

Thus, I am grateful to HarperCollins for my second chance. *Finding My Voice* is going to live again. New cover, but inside, the same sturdy machinery. There's mileage left, I believe, plenty of new readers to take along for the ride. And thanks to some people who cared as much as I do about this work, we will have a chance to find out.

Marie G. Lee is the author of *Finding My Voice*, *Saying Goodbye*, *Necessary Roughness*, and three other novels for young people. Her work has also appeared in the *Kenyon Review*, *American Voice*, and numerous anthologies. She was a Fulbright Scholar in creative writing to Korea and has taught literature at Yale University. Currently she is a Visiting Scholar in the American Civilization Department at Brown University.

Index

A Child Called "It," 101
ALA Best Books. *See* American Library Association Best Books
ALAN. *See* Assembly on Literature for Adolescents of NCTE
Alex Icicle: A Romance in Ten Torrid Chapters, 49, 78
All Quiet on the Western Front, 37, 39
American Library Association Best Books, 5, 68, 86, 87, 100, 121, 128
Angus, Thongs and Full-Frontal Snogging: Confessions of Georgia Nicolson, 49
Annie on My Mind, 108
The Arizona Kid, 48
Assembly on Literature for Adolescents of the National Council Teachers of English, xv, 7, 26, 30, 41, 54, 56, 84, 97, 120

Belden, Trixie, xvii, 31–36
Black Jack, 11, 13–14
Blinded by the Light, 116–19
Blume, Judy, 98, 100, 108
Bodart, Joni Richards, xvii, 100, 103, 107

Bode, Janet, xvii, 27–30
Bradford, Richard, xvii, 22, 25
Brancato, Robin, 116–18
Breaktime, xvii, 79–84
Bridgers, Sue Ellen, xvi, xvii, 17, 21, 51, 53–55
Brokaw, Tom, 37, 39–40
Bruises, 101

Cages of Glass, Flowers of Time, 98–101
Campbell, Patty, 1, xiii, xvi
Carroll, Pamela Sissi, xvii, 63, 67
Cart, Michael, xvi, xviii, 6, 9–10
The Catalogue of the Universe, xvii, 93–97
Catch-22, 25–26
The Catcher in the Rye, 25–26, 48
Chambers, Aidan, xvii, 79–83
The Chief, 9
The Chosen, 25
Christenbury, Leila, xvii, 68, 72
Christy, 21
Clements, Bruce, xvii, 73–78
Cold Mountain, 21
The Contender, 8, 25
Cormier, Robert, xvi, 98
Counterfeit Son, 99

Crosses, xvii, 112–15
Crowe, Chris, xvii, 22, 26
Culin, Charlotte, 98, 100–101

Daniel, Patricia L., xvii, 121, 125
Davis, Jenny, xvii, 42
Dobrez, Cindy, xvii, 98, 102
Donelson, Kenneth L., xvii, 50, 73, 78
Don't Hurt Laurie, 101
Don't You Dare Read This, Mrs. Dunphrey, 99
Dreamland, 45, 114

The Facts Speak for Themselves, 114
Fallen Angels, 37
Finding My Voice, 127–29
Ford, Margaret L., xvii, 57, 62
Forever, 108–9

Garfield, Leon, xvi, 11–15, 77
Go Ask Alice, 113
Good Night, Mr. Tom, 99

Hard Times: A Real Life Look at Juvenile Crime and Violence, 27–29
Harris and Me: A Summer Remembered, 48
Hipple, Ted, xvii, 79, 84
Hogan, William, 103, 106
Home Before Dark, xvii, 21, 51–55
Hubert, Jennifer, xvii, 108, 111
Hughes, Monica, xvii, 68–71

I Hadn't Meant to Tell You This, 64–65
I Tell a Lie Every So Often, 73–75, 77
If I Love You, Am I Trapped Forever?, 48–49
In Summer Light, 121–24

John Diamond, 11, 13
Jones, Patrick, xvii, 112, 115

Kate and the Revolution, 78
Kaywell, Joan F., xvii, 121, 125
The Keeper of the Isis Light, xvii, 68–72
Kelly, Patricia P., xvii, 93, 97
Krull, Kathleen, xvii, 31, 33, 36

The Last Mission, xvii, 37–40
Lee, Marie G., xvi, 126–29
Lee, Mildred, xvii, 17–21
Lesesne, Teri, xvii, 27, 29–30
Lipsyte, Robert, xvi, 6–10
Listen for the Fig Tree, xvii, 63–67
The Lottery Rose, 101

The Magician, xvii, 57–61
Mahy, Margaret, xvii, 93–94, 97
Make Lemonade, 5, 64
Marks, Bobby, 6–9
Mathis, Sharon, Bell, xvii, 63–67
Mazer, Harry, xvii, 37–40
Mazer, Norma Fox, xvii, 64, 108–11
Moore, John Noell, xvii, 37, 41
Myers, Walter Dean, 37, 39, 65

Naylor, Phyllis Reynolds, xvii, 88–92
Nilsen, Alleen Pace, xvii, 46, 50, 78
Noah's Castle, 1–5

One Fat Summer, 6–7
Oneal, Zibby, xvii, 121–22, 124
Oral History, 21
The Outsiders, 25

Paterson, Katherine, xvi, 11, 16, 39
The People Therein, 17, 19–21
The Pigman, 25
Plunking Reggie Jackson, 114
The Prisoner of Zenda, 78

The Quartzsite Trip, 103–06

The Red Badge of Courage, 39
Red Sky at Morning, xvii, 22–26
Ryan, Pam Muñoz, xvii, 85, 87

Salvner, Gary, xv
Say Goodnight, Gracie, 45
The Secret Diary of Adrian Mole Aged 13¾, xvii, 46–50
Send No Blessings, 88, 91–92
Sex Education, xvii, 42–45
Sheila's Dying, xvii, 85–87
The Skating Rink, 18–19
SLAM!, 65
Smack, 114
Small, Robert C., xvii, 116, 120
Smith, 11, 14–15
The Snarkout Boys and the Avocado of Death, 49
Sooner Later, 108
Speak, 45, 114
Staying Fat for Sarah Byrnes, 99
Stein, Sol, xvii, 57–61
Stevens, Susan L., xvii, 57, 62
Stoehr, Shelley, xvii, 112, 114–15
Stover, Lois, T., xvii, 88, 92
The Strange Affair of Adelaide Harris, 11–13, 77
Suds, 78
Summer Rules, 6–9
The Summerboy, 6–9

Talbert, Marc, xii
Tangerine, 65

Taylor, Mildred D., 26, 65
The Tempest, 122–24
To Kill a Mockingbird, 59
Toning the Sweep, 65
Townsend, John Rowe, xvi, 1, 4–5, 78
Townsend, Sue, xvii, 46–48
The Treasure of Plunderell Manor, 73, 75–78
Trust and Betrayal: Real-Life Stories of Friends and Enemies, 27–28

Under the Blood Red Sun, 39
Up in Seth's Room, 108–11

The Voices of Rape, 27–28

Weetzie Bat, 49
What Jamie Saw, 99
When She Was Good, 64
Wilder, Ann, xvii, 42, 45
The Window, 65
Wolff, Virginia Euwer, xvi, 1, 5, 64

YALSA. *See* Young Adult Library Services Association
The Year of Sweet Senior Insanity, 108
The Year of the Gopher, 88–92
You Don't Know Me, 99
Young Adult Library Services Association, xv, 10

Zitlow, Connie S., 51, 56

About the Editor

Connie S. Zitlow is a professor at Ohio Wesleyan University where she teaches courses in young adult literature, content area reading, and teaching methods. A former high school and middle school English and music teacher, she is now the director of Ohio Wesleyan's secondary education program. Her publications about young adult literature have appeared in numerous books and journals, and she served as the 2000 president of ALAN. A previous editor of the *Ohio Journal of the English Language Arts,* she is the current editor of the "Professional Links" column for *English Journal.*